Wood's

Wood's Illustrated Hand-Book to New York and Environs

A Guide for the Traveller or Resident ..

Wood's

Wood's Illustrated Hand-Book to New York and Environs
A Guide for the Traveller or Resident ..

ISBN/EAN: 9783337208929

Printed in Europe, USA, Canada, Australia, Japan

Cover: Foto ©Andreas Hilbeck / pixelio.de

More available books at **www.hansebooks.com**

WOOD'S ILLUSTRATED

HAND-BOOK

TO

NEW YORK

AND ENVIRONS.

A GUIDE FOR THE TRAVELLER OR RESIDENT.

WITH

MINUTE INSTRUCTIONS FOR SEEING THE METROPOLIS IN ONE OR MORE DAYS.

TOGETHER WITH NUMEROUS VALUABLE HINTS TO VISITORS ON NEARLY EVERY TOPIC THAT ARISES UPON THE SUBJECT OF SIGHT-SEEING.

COPIOUSLY ILLUSTRATED,

With Original Drawings made expressly for the Work.

NEW YORK:

G. W. Carleton & Co., Publishers.

LONDON: S. LOW, SON & CO.

M.DCCC.LXXIII.

Entered according to Act of Congress, in the year 1873, by
G. W. CARLETON & CO.,
In the Office of the Librarian of Congress, at Washington.

MINIATURE HISTORY OF NEW YORK.

MANHATTAN or New York Island was discovered September 6, 1609, by a crew of five men from Hudson's vessel. In the year 1625 it was purchased by the Dutch from the Indians for twenty-four dollars, the contents of the Island then being estimated at 22,000 acres. In 1625 the first church built of wood was erected in the present Bridge street; the first English settlers arrived the same year. In 1638 tobacco was produced to a considerable extent on the Island. In 1643 the houses were mostly one-story cabins with roofs of straw and chimneys of wood. In 1648 a wooden wharf was completed on the East River, on the present line of Moore street, being a continuation of the first wharf constructed in the city. The first lawyer commenced practice in 1650; in 1652 the first public school was established. The first City Hall was built in 1653 at the head of Coenties Slip. In 1656 the city was first surveyed and the streets laid down on a map. In 1659 a foreign trade first allowed to merchants of the city. In the year 1665 the city was incorporated under the government of a mayor, alderman and sheriff. Streets first paved in 1676; average price of lots fifty dollars. Rents varied from twenty-five to one hundred dollars per annum, payable partly in trade. The Anneke Jans farm of modern notoriety was leased on a rental equivalent to forty dollars per year, the lessee also to build a barn in part payment. In 1667 there were 12 streets and 384 houses. The number of licensed taverns in 1677 was 14. In 1678 the shipping belonging to the city was three ships and fifteen sloops and barks. In 1693 the first printing press was established in the city by William Bradford. The streets cleaned by contract in 1695 for £30 per annum. The debit and credit account of the city income and expenditure, one hundred and sixty-two years ago, presents a curious comparison with that of the present day. The items of *outlay* in the year 1710 were as follows: for the City Watch, which consisted of four men who went about the town "crying the hour of the night and the state of the weather," annual expense thirty-six pounds, exclusive of fire and light in the watchhouse, and the cost of lanterns and hour-glasses (which then served the place of watches) for the watchmen. For the salary of the Town Clerk, twenty pounds per annum. For the salary of the City Marshal, ten pounds per annum. The City Treasurer received five per cent. commission on his receipts. Besides the above, there were no stated expenditures. The items of *income* were derived from the following sources: leases of Corporation lands, about fifty pounds; liquor licenses, fifty-one pounds; fees for granting citizens' licenses of trade, ten pounds; and licenses to gaugers, four pounds. Rent of the Long Island ferry, one hundred and eighty pounds. In 1711 a *slave market* was established in Wall street; in 1729 three-pence a foot was given for land on the west side of Broadway, near the Battery. The first stage route between New York and Boston was established in 1732; time, 14 days from city to city. The first Merchants' Exchange established in 1752. When the British evacuated the city, November 25, 1783, the buildings did not extend beyond Murray street. In 1801 Broadway was ordered to be continued through Thomas Randall's land, near 8th street, to meet the Bowery. Previous to this extension of Broadway, the Bowery was the only entrance into the city, through groves of cedar, to the Bull's Head, now the Bowery Theatre. The old Potter's Field is now Washington Parade Ground. In 1806 there were two ferries to Brooklyn: one from Fly Market slip, now the foot of Maiden Lane, and one from Catherine slip; also there was a ferry to Paulus Hook, now Jersey City. These ferries were by row-boats, barges, and lighters. In 1807 Robert Fulton made his first trip to Albany in the first steamboat he built, called the Clermont; time, 32 hours. In April, 1807, there were only four Banks in the city.

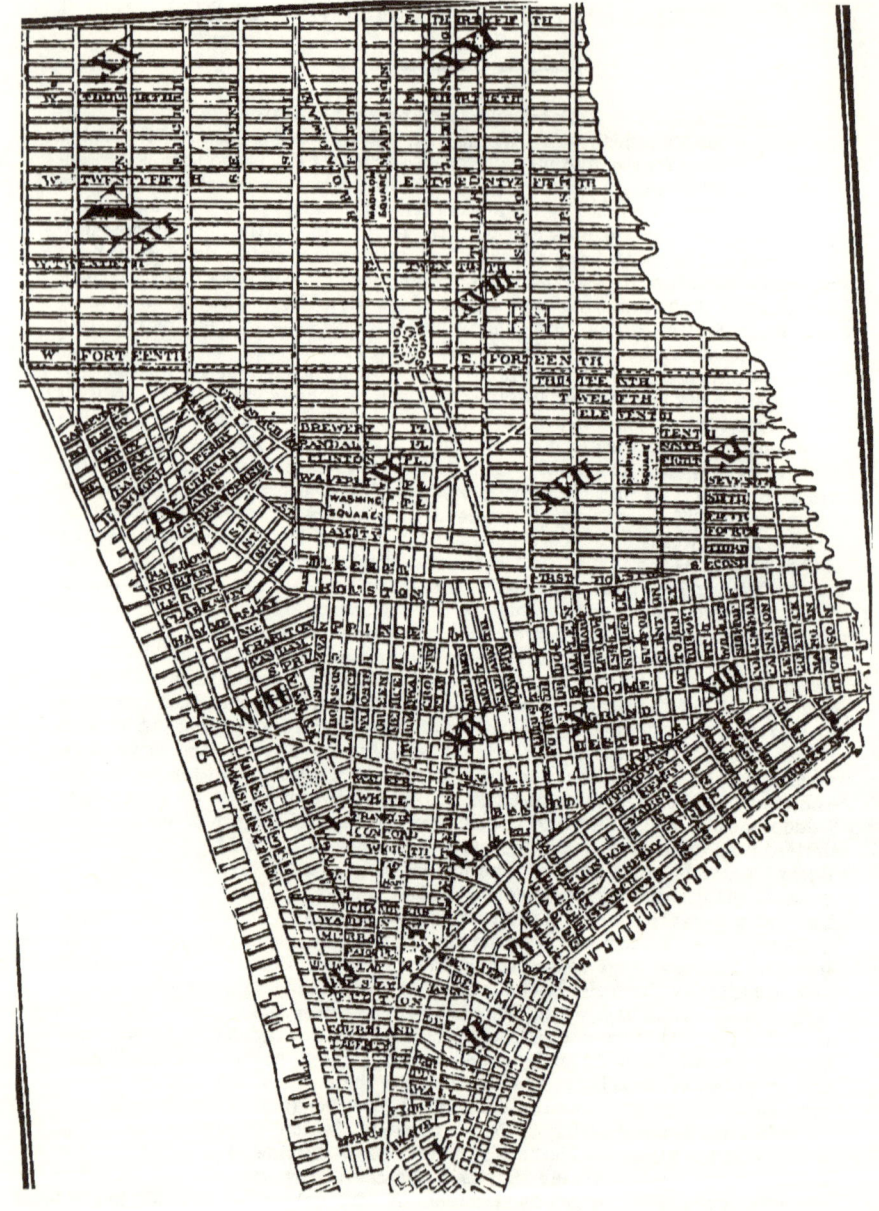

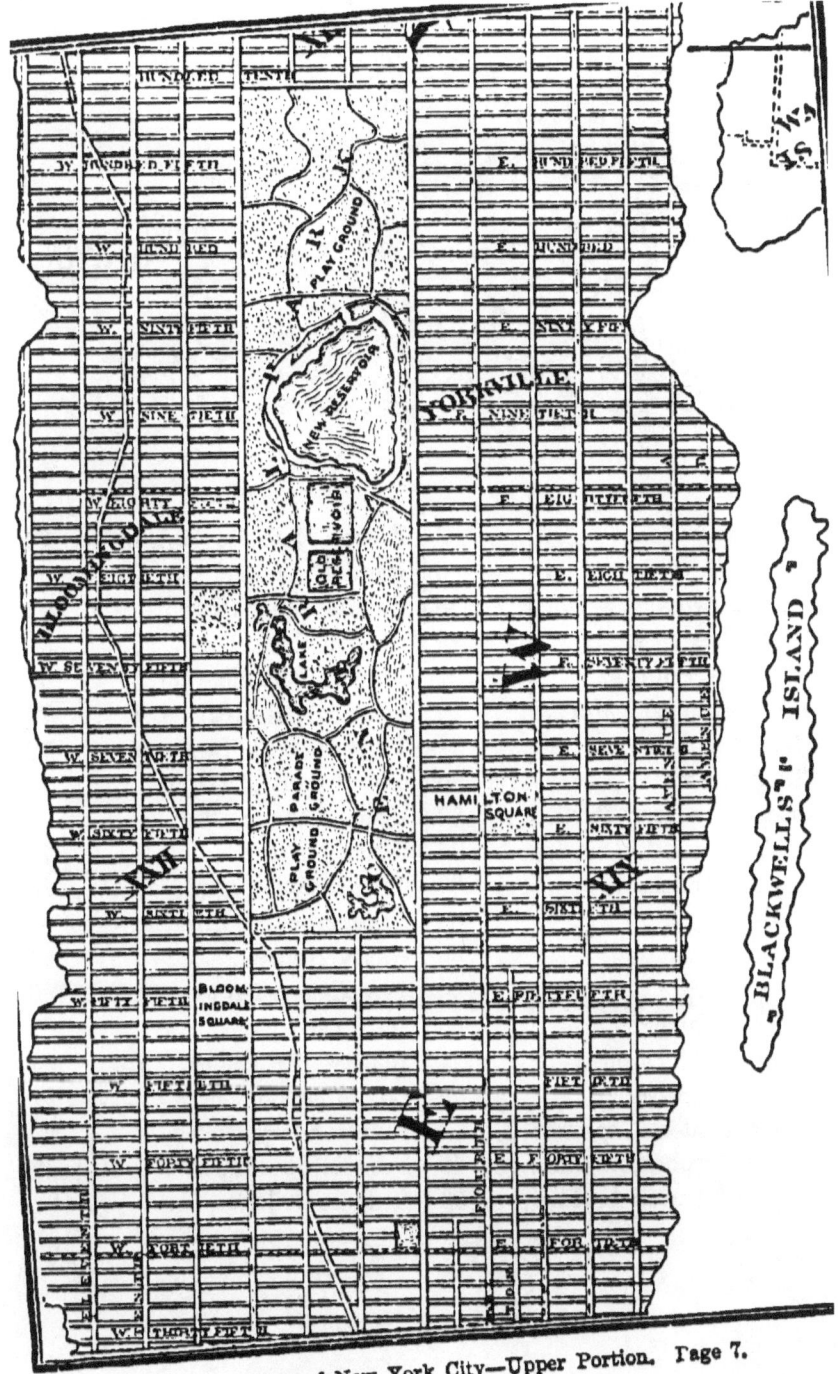

Map of New York City—Upper Portion.

List of Illustrations.
Drawn & Engraved by Fay & Cox, New-York City.

	PAGE		PAGE
Bird's-eye View	2	Roman Catholic Asylum	60
Map of New York City	6	Randall's Island	62
Coat of Arms New York	8	Sailors' Snug Harbor, S. I.	63
Castle Garden and Battery	19	Clinton Hall	65
Southern Point of N. Y.	21	Roman Catholic College	67
Old Washington Market	26	Seamen's Retreat, S. I.	70
Billiard Saloon	27	Third Ave. R. R. Depot	72
The Narrows	30	Grand Central Depot	74
Astor House and Park	32	Union League Club	76
A. T. Stewart's Charity	35	Grace Church	78
The Omnibuses	37	Jewish Synagogue	80
Madison Square	39	Knickerbocker Life Ins. Co.	82
Stock Exchange	45	Gilsey House	84
Astor Library	46	Fire Department	86
Booth's Theatre	50	Old Post-Office	87
Academy of Design	54	Blackwell's Island	89
Cooper Institute	56	Columbia College	91
Department of Charities	57	Fulton Ferry House	92
Colored Orphan Asylum	58	Fort Richmond, S. I.	95
Deaf and Dumb Asylum	59	Rutgers College	98

LIST OF ILLUSTRATIONS.   ix

	PAGE		PAGE
Fifth Avenue	99	Deaf and Dumb Asylum	134
The Grand Hotel	100	Barnum's Museum	138
Bible House	103	Convent of Sacred Heart	144
Egyptian Museum	105	Hell Gate Excavations	150
Society Library	107	Steam Fire Engine	155
Historical Society	109	The Morgue	157
Harlem Dispensary	110	Trinity Church Yard	162
St. Luke's Hospital	112	St. Paul's Church Yard	163
Seventh Regiment Armory	113	Trinity Church Yard	164
College of New York	115	Flower Girl	168
Croton Reservoir	117	Franklin Monument	169
Croton High Bridge	118	Café Brunswick	170
Navy Yard, Brooklyn	121	Jerome Park Races	172
Produce Exchange	124	Bethel Church	174
Battery Park	127	Blind Asylum	180
Washington Monument	128	Central Park, Summer H.	181
Lincoln Monument	129	Central Park, Lake	182
Mount Sinai Hospital	130	Central Park, Cave	183
New Post-Office	131	Central Park, Grotto	184
Tombs Prison	133	Lunatic Asylum	193

METHODICAL TABLE OF CONTENTS.

                                                                                    PAGE

1.—Alphabetical Index, - - - - -

2.—A Few Words about the City, - - - 19
    Giving a bird's-eye view of the Metropolis and its Inhabitants, and introducing the visitor to a literal acquaintance with the different phases of life and character to be found.

3.—Beware! - - - - - - - 27 ✓

4.—A separate Guide on opposite pages for Travellers arriving up-town and those arriving down-town, - - - - 30

5.—Narrative Guide, - - - - - 30
    The Tour of the City in half a day, one day, or more days.

6.—Amusements, - - - - - - 50

7.—Art Galleries, - - - - - - 54

8.—Asylums, - - - - - - - 57

9.—Benevolent Institutions, - - - - 61

10.—Benevolent Societies, - - - - 64

11.—Street Cars, - - - - - - 72

12.—Clubs, - - - - - - - 76

13.—Churches, - - - - - - - 78

	PAGE
14.—Companies,	82
15.—Consuls,	85
16.—Municipal Departments,	87
17.—Excursions,	89
18.—Ferries,	92
19.—Forts,	95
20.—Hacks, Coaches, Cabs, etc.,	97
21.—Hotels and Restaurants,	99
22.—Literary and Scientific Institutions,	10?
23.—Medical Institutions,	110
24.—Miscellaneous,	113
25.—Public Omnibuses,	126
26.—Parks and Squares,	127
27.—Public Buildings,	131
28.—Summer Resorts, and how to go to them,	135
29.—Hints and Notes on every variety of local matters,	137

    Including matters of dress, visits, and every item that the most inexperienced visitor to the City may require to know.

30.—The Central Park,	181
31.—Brief History of Old New York,	187
32.—Brooklyn and vicinity,	194
33.—Steamboat Travel,	198

ALPHABETICAL INDEX.

A.

A few Words about the City. 19
Advice to Travellers. 24
Additional Hints and Notes. 137
Amusements. 50
A New York Snow Storm. . 176
Armories of the City Militia. 113
Armories. . . . . . . ; 114
Asylums. 57
American Telegraph Co. . . . 83
Aqueducts. (See "Croton Water Works.") 117
Adjacent Islands. 61
Artists' Studios. 114
Art Galleries. 54
Avenues and Streets. 114
Associations. 64
Apprentices' Library. 102
A Lady may Wear— 137
Arrival in New York. 30
Area of the City. 19
American Museum of Art. . 55

B.

Banks. 116
Banks Open. 139
Benevolent Institutions. . . . 57
Benevolent Societies. 64
Baths—of all kinds. 116
Boarding Houses. 177
Billiards. 139
Breweries. . . . .

Bay of New York. 30
Buildings 159
Brooklyn 194
Barnum's Museum as it was 138
Bible House. 103
Blackwell's Island. 61
Beware! 27
Base Ball. 139
Boat Races. 139
Budget of New York. 139
Baths—Free Public. 116
Boulevards. 139

C.

Cars — *Street* and Omnibuses. 72
Courts. 142
Croton Water Works. 117
Churches 78
Corporation Library. 104
Cemeteries. 196
Consuls. 85
Clubs. 76
Choice of Locality. 143
Collections of Objects of Art. 142
Commerce, Industry, and Immigration. 140
Custom House Dues. 141
Courts Open. 142
Colleges. 142
City Statistics. 139

Cabs 97
Confectioneries 116
Courts open to the Public. 142
Carts and Cartmen 142
Colored Relief 66
Calls and Callers, and How
 to Dress 141
Central Park 181
Conservatories of Music ... 50
Clinton Hall 104
Chop Houses 99
City Hall 131
Commercial Register 117
Club Houses, how to be seen 77
Custom House Regulations. 141
Calls after Dinner 145
City Directory 144

Elevators 145
East River 90
English Sparrows in the
 Squares, and their Habi-
 tations 21
Express Offices 83
Express—how to send by.. 84
Emigrants' Landing Depot. 153
Evening Newspapers 168
Excursion Boats 198
Egyptian Museum. See
 "Historical Society".... 105

D.

Description of the City.... 19
Departments 87
Dispensaries 111
Detectives 145
Docks 119
Distances across the Ferries. 143
Directory 144
Dinner Hour and after Din-
 ner Visits 145
Dinners, public and private;
 where to give them 99
Daily Newspapers 168
Drinking Saloons 144
Distances in the City 143

E.

Excursions 89
Effects of a New York Snow
 blockade 176

F.

Fund Societies—are in al-
 phabetical order in "Be-
 nevolent Societies." See
 Index 64
Ferries and Piers 92
Fashion Plates 145
Fashionable Dress Makers. 145
Free Academy 104
Forts 95
French Cooking 145
Ferries to Brooklyn 93
Freemasons 67
Foreign Money 146
Fashionable Day for Ladies 145
Fashionable Newspapers... 146
French and German Waiters 146
Furnished Apartments..... 146
Furnished Houses 146
Fruit Stores 146
Fashionable Patterns of all
 kinds for Ladies' and
 Children's Garments.... 145
Fashion 145

G.

Great Thoroughfares...... 147
German and Swedish Immigration.............. 146
Gambling Houses and Decoys................... 148
German Music Halls or Reunions................ 52
Greenwood................ 196
Gymnasiums............... 148
Grocery Stores............ 147
Government Warehouses.. 141

H.

Hell Gate and the East River Improvements, and their probable effect in changing the business localities................. 149
How to Descend from a Car or Omnibus when you wish to................. 153
How to see a Newspaper. See "Reading Rooms" in Index................... 153
Hotel Coaches............. 151
How to Stop a Stage or Car when you wish to get out 148
How to get a Newspaper... 153
How to see New York Quickly................. 24
How to see New York Leisurely.................. 38
Hints to Visitors in the Metropolis. See "Hints and Notes"................... 137
Holidays in New York..... 151
Hudson River............. 90
Harlem River............. 149

History of New York...... 187
How to Stop a Stage or Car where you wish to get out 153
Hacks and Hackmen....... 97
Hotels and Restaurants for all respectable persons according to their means.. 99
Help for Educated but Poor Girls from the Country.. 68
Howard Mission for Little Wanderers.............. 68
How to Catch a Train in a hurry.................. 153
Hints on Accepting Invitations.................. 149
How to Dress at Operas and Theatres, and other places of amusement. See Index for "Amusements".. 51

I.

Illustrated Newspapers.... 168
If you leave an article in an Omnibus or Car........ 153
Infirmary................. 58
Ice Water................. 153
If you choose to see to your own Baggage........... 153
If you are Invited to an Entertainment............ 149
Information Bureau for Friends of Arriving Immigrants................ 153
Immigration.............. 153
Immigration—Comparative Protestant and Catholic. 155

J.

Jerome Park............. 173

L.

Letters 155
Literary and Scientific Institutions 102
Libraries. (See Index for Literary and Scientific Institutions.) 102
Length of Blocks 143
Long Branch Steamers 203
Ladies' Depository. (Reduced Ladies.) 69
Letter Stamps 155
Laborers 156
List of Engravings 7
Letter Boxes 155

M.

May Anniversaries 156
Moving Day in the Metropolis 158
Measures of Length 159
Medical Institutions 110
Mock Auctions 28
Map of the City ....
Miscellaneous 113
Map of Brooklyn ....
Miscellaneous Exhibitions.. 135
Messengers 156
Mayor's Office 88
Modes of Visiting Separate Places on the Hudson... 91
Mechanics' Society School. 106
Markets 120
Matinees 175
Morgue 157
Musical Matters. (See Index for "Amusements" and under "Literary and Scientific Institutions"... 50

Municipal Division of the City 158
Measures of Capacity 159
Money 119

N.

Navy Yard 120
Naval Dry Dock 119
Newspapers 168
New York Fashionable Season 24
Narrows 30
National Academy of Design 54
Novelty Works 120
No Rule for Business Office Hours 139
North, East, and Harlem Rivers and Sound Boats. 198
Natural Flowers 167
New Buildings 159
Narrative Guide 30
New York Yacht Club 77
New York City Taxes for 1872 166

O.

Organ Grinders and Street Beggars 28
Offices or Bureaus are in alphabetical order in "Miscellaneous" 113
Opera 51
Omnibuses and Cars 126
Odd-Fellows 69
Out-door Statues and Monuments 128

P.

Public Lectures	53
Public Instruction	161
Public Buildings	131
Parks and Squares	127
Public Schools	161
Postage	120
Public Schools,—how they are built, arranged, and conducted	161
Postal Arrangements	121
Public Porters	122
Police	88
Police Stations	122
Police Courts	88
Picture Galleries—public	54
Picture Galleries—private	55
Post-office	131
Population of the City	19
Popular Preachers	196
Places and Sights which a Stranger should see	90
Printing House Square	123
Publishing Offices	123
Piers and Ferries	92
Public and Private Dinners	145
Photography	54
Police Protection and Detective Department	88
Police Telegraph	88

R.

Resorts at short distances from Town	135
Resorts for Evenings. (See Index for "Amusements.")	50
Railroad Stations	124
Rides and Drives	89
Reservoirs. (See Index for "Croton Water Works.")	117
Races	172
Re-unions—German	52
Restaurants	99
Riding School	173
Reading and Smoking Rooms	153
Religion	173
Routine to make the Travellers' sight-seeing delightful and not trying and exhausting to mind and body	45
Religious Newspapers	173
Religious Notes	173
The tour of the City in half a day	38

S.

Servants	156
Summer Resorts, or Watering Places at a distance, and how to go to them	135
Schools—public	161
Shop Butchers	175
Streets and Avenues	143
Steamboats	198
Saturday	175
Silver Communion Service, presented by Queen Anne	175
Safe Deposit Companies	124
Sunday Services	196
Study of Students in Art	54
Something for the Antiquary	191
Stewart's Store	123
Society for the Prevention of Cruelty to Animals	71
Stevens Apartment Building	38
Salaries of Public Employés	166
Sailors' Snug Harbor	64
Sailors' Chapels	175

Shopping.................... 175
Shipping Intelligence....... 177
Seeing to your own baggage 153
Shipping in the Harbor.... 22
Sites of remarkable events. 191
Suburban Trains or Railroads................. 124
Suburban Railroad Stations 135
Suburban Villages.......... 177
Shooting Galleries......... 175
Seamen's Exchange........ 123
Sum total of business transacted in the City of New York in 1871. (See "Commerce and Industry.").. 141
Summer..................... 136

T.

Trip up the Hudson........ 90
The Police................. 88
Table of Distances......... 179
Theatres 51
The New York Bar......... 108
Telegraphy................. 83
Telegraph Offices.......... 125
Take the Right-hand....... 177
Traffic.................... 208
The Churches.............. 78
Tides...................... 208
Time Tables............... 178
Telegraph Companies...... 83
Thermometric Scale...... 159
Trips...................... 90
The Tombs, or City Prison 133
To hear Trials............. 142
Those who wish to remain in New York as Students, Clerks, &c.............. 34
There are no American Servants................... 156
To Philadelphia, Baltimore, and Washington........ 198

The Tour of the City in one day..................... 39
The Tour of the City in three or more days...... 38
To give an idea of the fashionable watering places frequented by New Yorkers..................... 89

U.

United States Treasury.... 134
Unfurnished Apartments.. 178

V.

Views of New York....... 125

W.

Weights and Measures..... 159
Width of Streets and Avenues................... 143
Wall Street................. 40
Wall Street Sneak Thieves. 180
Where to Lunch, Dine, and Sup.................... 99
Wharves and Wharf Scenes. 125
Working Girls' Hotel...... 35
What to beware of........ 29
What can be bought in Broadway............... 125
Woodlawn................. 106
Waiters in Hotels......... 180
Washington............... 128
Wines and Liquors....... 180

Y.

Yachting 77
Religious Statistics for the United States.......... 173

HANDBOOK OF NEW YORK.

A FEW WORDS ABOUT THE CITY.

[*Castle Garden, at the Battery.*]

NEW YORK stands at the head of the magnificent bay of the same name, seventeen miles from the Atlantic Ocean. Into the bay flows on one side of the city the East river, and on the other the Hudson or North river. The Harlem river and Spuyten Duyvil creek make the northern boundary, and complete the island, which is the limit of the city proper.

Its shape is long and narrow, with an average width of a mile and a half; and its principal street—Broadway—extends its entire length, a distance of fifteen miles. The population is over one million, not taking into account that of Brooklyn, Jersey City, and the contiguous places in Westchester county, which would increase it to about a million and three-quarters.

The growth of New York is amazing, the last few years witnessing the rapid extension of streets from river to river, and the opening of broad avenues northward, far beyond the city boundaries.

The advance of New York has been remarkable ever since the Revolution, the events and peculiarities which make history seeming to have no limit in the variety and perpetuity of their striking elements.

The climate, though variable, is extremely healthy. Fogs never obscure the heavenly blue skies, and such weather as Nature sends has a poetic beauty, whether in sunshine or storm. Here are found the exhilaration of the Russian winter, the balmy influence of the tropical summer, and the incomparable spring and autumn seasons peculiar to the northern United States. The lavish supply of pure water distributed by the Croton Aqueduct is its chief artificial sanitary arrangement. This is at the command of all, rich and poor. It is carried into every house, however insignificant, and distributed through it from top to bottom in pipes let into the walls and turned out by faucets, with larger pipes to carry off the waste water.

The sewage of the whole metropolis is conducted into the Hudson and East rivers through brick tunnels which underlie the streets. No drainage is necessary into those wide rivers which communicate with the ocean and are salt.

The breezes which sweep from the ocean through these noble rivers and along the streets, temper the rigor of the winters, and cool the sultry heats of summer. As the streets run from river to river, the air has free scope in carrying away malaria and the foul odors due to neglectful city authorities, and serve to mitigate the fiercest ravages of disease in seasons of epidemic.

The parks and squares are delightful breathing spots. Unenclosed and beautifully paved, they are peculiarly inviting. They are planted with trees, and have beautifully kept grass-plots and admirable walks and inviting seats. They are filled with English sparrows (imported for the protection of the trees against the caterpillars); and in Madison and Union Squares are ingeniously contrived miniature buildings for these little birds, placed among the branches of the trees, which represent different business departments, as "The Post-Office," "The Custom-House," "The Exchange," &c., &c., &c., and it is very amusing to see the little creatures enter these different edifices, their busy, hurried air irresistibly giving the idea that they really know where they are going and have a purpose in it.

It will strike a stranger how infinitely greater is the proportion of respectable and elegant streets, and how comparatively limited are those absorbed by poverty and vice. If he has time for investigation he will learn also how ample are the provisions for the extinction of the latter. There is no city in the world where there are so many charitable institutions of all kinds.

The northern or upper part of the city is appropriated to private life; the lower or southerly portion to commerce,

[*The Southern Point of New York.*]

traffic, and law. Wealth, taste, and ambition are stamped upon the streets devoted to business as fully as upon those designed expressly for luxury and ease. Warehouses are nowhere shut in by dingy, unwholesome alleys, but are in every street lighted by the bright sunshine; and the "dark ways," if there are any, are confined to interior transactions. Commerce at and near the wharves is carried on in the unobscured light of day, which gives the cheerfulest aspect to all concerned, and an infinite animation to the varied and ever-changing scenes.

Along the Hudson and East rivers can be seen almost the largest display of shipping in the world. For several miles you behold literally a "forest of masts."

The city is full of public schools, where the best English education can be had free.

The intellectual quickness produced by the rapidity of New York life, renders the corps of lawyers quite independent of the seclusion of a London "Lincoln's Inn" or a "Temple." In New York, commerce and law are found in close juxtaposition.

Retail trade, on the other hand, has scarcely a foothold in the so-called business part of the city, but is scattered about in the great thoroughfares with a judicious adaptation of the quality of the merchandise to the quality of the neighborhood.

Fortunate business and professional men, retired men of wealth, in short, millionaires—whether they have made their money in the retail trade or at wholesale, whether as mechanics or lawyers, bankers or brokers, as doctors or as clergymen, so long as the money *is* made—buy lots and build magnificent houses in the most fashionable streets. The "born gentleman," with a long pedigree and a lean purse, will find scanty recognition there. Indeed there is probably a greater social distinction in some of the business quarters of the city between the different occupations, than in the private portions of the metropolis, where the only distinguishing features are the different degrees of wealth displayed.

In New York there is no technical division between the business and the private portion of the town. It is all the 'city." "We are going to the 'city'"—"We have been to the 'city'"—"We have business in the 'city'"—means New York, and not as in London only a small part of the metropolis.

The expressions "down town" and "up town" are employed to designate the business and social quarters of the city. There is no confusion in New York, as in London, from many streets bearing the same name.

The government of New York is vested in the Mayor and Board of Aldermen and Assistant Aldermen, with a vast machinery of branches, from the city Comptroller down. There are also various departments, such as the "Department of Public Works," the "Department of Public Charities and Correction," &c., which to an extent are independent in their working, and which serve to increase the confusion in the management of the city's affairs. It is to be hoped that a comprehensive and intelligible charter will in time be enacted, which will enable New Yorkers to escape from the official thieves and robbers who have of late so audaciously plundered them.

The active, cheerful labor which is shared by all classes, each in their specific sphere, the HOPE which the unlimited facilities for enterprises of all kinds stamp upon every countenance, the bearing, imbued with conscious independence, all render the New Yorker an eminent example of the true type of republican character.

Here every nationality on the face of the earth would appear to be represented. This large influx of foreigners, who adopt New York for their home, while they introduce many of the habits and customs of their native land, quickly imbibe the spirit of our free institutions and become rapidly Americanized. This makes the city thoroughly Cosmopolitan.

The city of New York is the head-quarters of the trade and commerce of the United States. It is also the nucleus of all southern and western travel in the summer season. A peculiar feature of New York is the multiplicity of fashionable hotels and boarding-houses. These are sustained to a great degree by the "respectability" of the metropolis. This is partly owing to the want of good servants (a great want), partly to the fact that only persons of large incomes can pay the enormous rents for private houses, it being a rule of "good society" that every family must live in a *whole house* (if they keep house at all); and fashion, arbitrary here as elsewhere, compels people hoping to maintain their position to live in a large and handsome house, however small their family may be. Hence, hotel and boarding-house life has been reduced to a fine art.

It is getting to be much the custom for families who are so fortunate as to own splendid houses on the avenues, and who lack somewhat the means to support these establishments, to live almost wholly at their suburban residences, which, as a rule, are very fine, and come in the city to a hotel at their convenience and pleasure, while the town house, with all its rich furniture, is let to a "fashionable" boarding-house keeper.

Fashionable New York usually quits town for the country in June, and returns in October. Before the civil war the city was none the less gay for the flight of its inhabitants to cooler regions. The southern planters came north with their families, flocking like tropical birds of brilliant plumage to the hotels, fluttering along the walks, and keeping the sultry streets full of life and brightness. They come still, those who can; but they have no longer the inclination nor the means for their former display.

The most fashionable period at the chief summer resorts is the last week of July and the first two weeks in August.

The fashionable season in the city is from early in November to Lent.

The first impulse of a stranger in coming into a metropolis is to consult a map. But the visitor who is limited for time will find it to his advantage to follow a little "*tour*" marked out for him in the narrative part of the "HANDBOOK," a perusal of which will take but a few minutes. It has been planned with study and care, and will be found very comprehensive and satisfactory. Afterwards, the map will come in use. The "tour" gives an exterior view of the most beautiful and the most characteristic portions of the metropolis, with their architectural features, and many buildings which are pointed out by name. The most busy as well as the most fashionable portions are included.

In passing through the business thoroughfares the visitor will find the striking peculiarities of our American life agglomerated with almost a weird effect. He will find palatial banks and banking houses, immense insurance buildings, lawyers' offices, brokers' offices in great variety, enormous wholesale stores of every possible description, spacious government warehouses, towering newspaper offices, and innumerable hotels, mixed up with restaurants, lunch-rooms, cigar-shops, wine and fruit stores, a few churches, and large numbers of second-hand book stores; while along the streets are innumerable stands, where newspapers and light literature are dispensed, or oranges, apples, bananas, in fact all the fruits of the season, are sold, together with roasted chestnuts, peanuts, crockery, new and second-hand clothing, &c., &c.; while far "up town" stretch rows of private houses, interspersed with churches, hotels, boarding-houses, fashionable restaurants, and confectionery establishments.

The markets are interesting places to visit, especially early in the morning, before the full tide of traffic is begun. The varieties of home produce, the great market-baskets of fruits and vegetables, the game, the live poultry, the heaps of eggs, the bunches of flowers and of herbs, the huge, ruddy-faced, bright market women who reign over their stalls, inviting by

[*Old Washington Market.—Morning.*]

word and glance the new comer, or welcoming with the freedom of their class the old-established customer, with offers of bargains mingled with the witty remark and the sharp but good-humored repartee—all these form a scene and a picture which should not be overlooked.

It is much the custom in New York for gentlemen, and often ladies, to go themselves to market to make their purchases for the day's requirements.

And now we introduce the reader to New York, as beyond question one of the freshest, liveliest, and most fascinating cities in the world.

BEWARE!

[*Scene in Billiard Saloon.*]

BEWARE—

On approaching and coming into the city, of the good-natured civilities of persons you have never seen before. Gratuitous offers of assistance or advice, or good-fellowship, are suspicious, to say the least.

Do not be persuaded to go anywhere with these casual acquaintances. If you are an utter stranger, you will find the "Handbook" your best and most trustworthy friend. It will not mislead you. While it is not necessary to particularize every place in the metropolis that is respectable as a stopping-place, or as a resort for amusement, it leaves unmentioned such as are in the least doubtful, and which ought to be avoided. Some which are notorious and extremely insidious, are briefly specified under this heading, while the newspapers give daily accounts of the innumerable ways of entrapping strangers in the city.

BEWARE—

If you are at a loss in the street, of accosting any one but a policeman; him you will know by his uniform—blue coat and cap, and brass buttons. If you do not see a policeman, step into the nearest store or hotel and make your inquiries.

Beware—

Of the purlieus of the city. They are only to be visited under the escort of a police officer.

Beware—

Of Mock Auctions in stores, and of the pleasant-faced man who invites you to look in.

Beware—

Of Panel Houses. A sliding panel is let into the walls of some doubtful houses, through which thieves enter unperceived and have you at their mercy.

Beware—

Of Saloons with "Pretty Waiter Girls." They are among the most dangerous decoys in the city.

Beware—

Of all who accost you in the street, particularly if they want your advice about a pocket-book they have just found, or a roll of money which they have picked up. Such persons have a very innocent and inexperienced air. Distrust them—don't stop to listen to them.

Beware—

Of visiting a fashionable gambling-house, "just to see what is going on."

Beware—

Of giving street beggars or organ-grinders more than a few pennies.

Beware—

Of walking late in the evening, except in the busiest thoroughfares of the city.

Beware—

Of exposing your watch, pocket-book, or jewelry in the

streets, lecture-rooms, theatres, or in omnibuses or cars. You should suspect any one, man or woman, well or ill dressed, who *crowds* or presses against you; the contents of your pockets are in danger. Ladies, keep your pocket-books in the bosom of your dress.

BEWARE—

Of Hack-drivers' extortions. (See index for "Hacks and Hackmen.")

BEWARE—

Of passing under a building in course of erection or repairs. It is worth while to cross the street twice to avoid it.

BEWARE—

Especially in the evening, of persons who ask you what time it is. They have designs on your watch.

BEWARE—

Of leaving any considerable sum of money or any valuables in your trunk, or of carrying them on your person. There is a safe in every hotel where you can deposit such things without charge.

BEWARE—

Of talking about your business before strangers.

BEWARE—

Of even the *orderly* "Dance-Houses." A sadder story of New York life cannot be written than that connected with these places.

NARRATIVE GUIDE.

[*The Narrows, at Fort Hamilton.*]

THOSE who, for the first time, sweep up our magnificent BAY, pass the brilliant "NARROWS," and reach the city at its lower extremity, and those who arrive by the numerous steamboat lines, or who alight from the various routes of travel at the stupendous "GRAND CENTRAL DEPOT" at Forty-second Street, will naturally wish for a thorough but concise and lucid GUIDE to not only the most convenient or accessible HOTELS, but also to CHURCHES of all denominations, the THEATRES, OPERA HOUSES, MUSEUMS, PUBLIC LIBRARIES, and the most eligible RETAIL STORES. They will also desire to be guided in their strolls about town.

The more necessary landmarks being well fixed in the mind, Public Institutions of all kinds, Public Buildings, and private streets of note will come next in interest. The channels which lead out of the city then occupy the attention, and the traveller feels quite at home.

He can now *observe* without the hurry and excitement which always accompany *a sense of strangeness;* and whether his stay be for a few weeks, days, or only hours, he can *repose* while he contemplates the characteristics of the great metropolis of the Western World, and the peculiarities of its inhabitants as they are exhibited in their places of business, their homes, and their chosen pursuits and pleasures.

N. B. — Travellers arriving at either extremity of the metropolis will find separate instructions on opposite pages until it is time for them to join company.

TRAVELLER FROM DOWN-TOWN.

The stranger entering the metropolis from the Jersey Ferries, or by the Hudson and East Rivers, will find his way to his stopping-place by the aid of the HANDBOOK. (See Index for Hotels and Restaurants.)

Having consigned your baggage to the care of the express agent—who gives you a receipt, and whose "Company" is responsible for it until it safely reaches its destination; having paid your hackman (see Index for "Hackmen"), or, with carpet-bag in hand, having chosen to vary the boat or railroad motion by a brisk walk to your stopping-place, and taken your comfortable meal, reposed for a few moments in your apartment, or, if but a passing traveller, in the reading-room or the office of the hotel, or in your chair in the dining-room or restaurant, with the HANDBOOK before you, you are soon rested and armed for an excursion about the city.

If you have taken an apartment, we advise you to preface

your first meal by a bath and clean linen. Besides making you presentable wherever you may choose to go, it wonderfully accelerates the cheerful feeling which gives all the zest to sight-seeing.

If you have not engaged an apartment, you can still have the use of the toilet-room of the hotel with water, soap, and towels, and thus enjoy something of the invigoration of the bath.

[*Astor House—Broadway and Park Row.*]

I now propose a little tour. I shall make the ASTOR HOUSE the starting-point for the down-town sight-seer. (See Index for "Hotels.") If you arrive by one p.m. in winter, or by three p.m. at any other season, commence your sight-seeing by stepping from the Broadway door of the Astor House into a Fifth Avenue omnibus, going up town, or north. One passes every few minutes. This will carry you up Broadway to Eleventh Street, thence into the far-famed Fifth Avenue. Continue your ride up this avenue to the upper end of the "Reservoir," at Forty-second Street. Here alight, and walk one block in an easterly direction and you are at Madison Avenue, near the "Grand Central Depot," which occupies almost the whole block between Madison and Fourth Avenues. From here you take the "Tour" marked out for the sight-seer from "Up-Town." (See page   .) This tour will bring you to the corner of Broadway and Twenty-third Street, where take an omnibus and return down town to your stopping-place in time to rest, dress, and dine, and visit some evening place of amusement. The waiter at your chair will bring you a daily newspaper, if you have not already one in your possession, and you can make your choice of places of resort while you are sipping your coffee.

If you arrive by a morning boat I propose a different and much more comprehensive tour, as follows:

After breakfast, step into a Broadway and Wall Street omnibus, going down, or southerly. This will take you down Broadway a short distance, and then will turn into Wall Street, which is the famous money mart of the metropolis, and carry you to the Wall Street Ferry. The distance is not great, but as the streets are thronged, you can observe to better advantage from a slight elevation, and the ride will cost you but ten cents, which you hand up to the driver on entering the omnibus. At the head of Wall Street you will meet with the sight-seer from "up-town," and from this point you join company in all your excursions.

Traveller from "Up-Town."

On approaching the metropolis, an express agent passes through the cars, exclaiming "Checks for baggage." You will have made up your mind where you desire to go, and it will be wise to entrust your baggage to him. Accost him as he approaches. Tell him where you wish it taken—whether to another railroad depot, or to a steamboat (if you are only passing through town), or to some part of the city. He takes out his book, puts down your instructions; you deliver to him your checks, for which he gives you a receipt, and you have transferred all the care of your baggage to the express company, who are responsible for it until it is safely delivered. The express charge is half a dollar for each trunk.

On emerging from the immense Depot, you find yourself in Forty-second Street, facing the south or "down-town," with Madison Avenue on your right and Fourth Avenue on your left. If you are weary and travel-soiled, take a hack (see Index for "Hacks and Hackmen") for your place of destination; but if you have only a few hours to spend in the metropolis, and are a pretty good walker, I propose a short tour which will give you the best view of the most elegant part of the city at various points, with many buildings of note, and without greatly retracing your steps, which is the discouraging and time-stealing impediment to the sight-seer. The up-town streets are seen to much better advantage in walking than in riding.

Proceed, then, down Park Avenue (this is built over Fourth Avenue, the latter being used for a railroad tunnel), and walk leisurely straight before you to its termination at Thirty-second Street, where it is merged in Fourth Avenue. Park Avenue is one of the three most beautiful and fashionable avenues in the metropolis, and has been recently, and in an incredibly short time, built up over the Harlem Railroad tunnel. Here, at

[*A. T. Stewart's Working-Girls' Hotel.*]

Thirty-second Street, is A. T. Stewart's great charity, The Working-Girls' Hotel. If you want any articles of the toilet, thread, needles, pins, scissors, a thimble, a ribbon, a neck-tie, a comb and brush, etc., proceed a few blocks in the same direction along Fourth Avenue, and make the purchases at any of the stores whose windows exhibit such and similar articles. The few minutes you have spent in Fourth Avenue will be sufficient to give you an idea of the character of that thoroughfare, which, together with Third Avenue, is merged at Seventh Street in the broad highway called the Bowery, leading to the lower part of the city. You may now retrace your steps to the corner of Thirty-fourth Street, turn here to your left, or westerly, and one block brings you to Madison Avenue. Take a glance up and down its beautiful double line of private residences and pass on to the next crossing, and you are in the Fifth Avenue, and directly before you is the classical marble edifice built by A. T. Stewart, merchant, for his private residence. You have now seen from the best point of view the most fashionable avenues and several of the finest up-town streets of the metropolis, presenting, in their regular intersecsection, *façades* of unrivalled extent and beauty. Turn here at your left and walk down Fifth Avenue to Madison Square, pausing at the corner of Twenty-fifth Street to look about you. This is a short half mile farther. If it is afternoon and a fine day, you will meet the "belles" and "beaux" of New York in their elegant toilets, and have the advantage of a near inspection of the much-boasted beauty of the New York ladies; also of the brilliant display of equipages as they roll along, bearing their freight of wealth and fashion to Central Park. Giving a glance at the Worth Monument near which you are standing, walk to the lower or southern extremity of the square in Twenty-third Street, and you are at the intersection of Broadway with the Fifth Avenue, which is one of the finest points in the city. The view in every direction is imposing. Directly opposite, is the massive marble front of the Fifth Avenue Hotel, and in this vicinity are congregated a large number of the first-class hotels of the city. After taking a survey of the scene, turn to your left, or easterly, and walk one block, and you will find yourself at the corner of Fourth Avenue and Twenty-third Street. Here, standing opposite each other, are The National Academy of Design and the building of The Young Men's Christian Association. The exterior is all you have time to look at to-day. Retrace your steps, walking westerly past the lower side of Madison Square till you come again to Broadway.

[N.B.—If you have come in town, travelled, soiled, and weary, and *have another day* for sight-seeing, you will wish to proceed directly to your hotel; preface your first meal by a rapid bath; it wonderfully revivifies. There are barber shops and bath-rooms in all first-class hotels. At other houses, a bed-room with water and towels answer the purpose; in fact, this refreshment will be well worth the time in the rest it will give you and the zest it will add to your first venture at sight-seeing, even if you have but a few hours to spend in the metropolis.]

The next step, after once more pausing to admire the scene around you from where you stand—corner of Twenty-third Street and Broadway—is to consult your watch and see what time you have for further sight-seeing. If you have still an hour left, take a South Ferry Omnibus—"South Ferry" is painted on it in large letters—and ride down to the Bowling Green and return by another stage of the same line. This will give you a panoramic view of the whole of Broadway, with a glimpse of all the intersecting streets and of the Battery, and you will have had already a good view of New York.

You can now refresh yourself, dine, and attend some place of amusement in the evening.

If you have arrived by a morning train and have but a few hours in the city, proceed at once by taking the little tour just described.

If you have longer to stay, the first thing for you to do after comfortably arranging yourself at your hotel, is to sally forth and stop a Broadway and Wall Street Omnibus, going downtown or south. Stop it by raising your finger. There is generally a policeman in uniform at hand to help passengers across the streets when they are much crowded. Step into the omnibus and pass up your fare—*ten cents*. You will get correct change for any small bill, if necessary, though it is much more convenient to be prepared with the exact sum. For a distance of two or three miles you have nothing to do but admire the buildings which compose this splendid street.

On Broadway are most of the prominent hotels of the metropolis, all buildings of imposing structure and proportions. Here are theatres, museums, and an infinite number of magnificent edifices for merchandise, for offices, &c. Your omnibus does not go up Broadway above Twenty-third Street, but turns into Madison Avenue; therefore you should take it at this point, or below it. If you have chosen the Grand Hotel or any of the contiguous hotels for your stopping-place, you can readily walk down to Twenty-third Street. The Grand is the farthest north of a series of hotels. Starting from here, corner of Thirty-first Street, cross to the west side of Broadway, and you will see all the hotels to the best advantage. On the next block below, at your left hand, is the Gilsey House, also a beautiful building of more florid architecture. Near the corner of Thirtieth Street, at your right hand, is Wood's Museum; on the next block, at your left, is the Sturtevant House, and on your right, nearly opposite, is the Coleman House. A little farther on, at your left, is a large and striking building of brick, with stone facings; this is the new *Stevens Apartment Building*, constructed in "flats" for families, after the French style and in the most elegant manner.

At the corner of Twenty-fifth Street and Broadway pause a moment. From this point is one of the most beautiful views of the metropolis. Two blocks at your left, across Madison Square, is the showy and singular building of the Union League Club. On your right stretches a marble façade of several of the first-class hotels. The first of these white marble buildings is the St. James Hotel, which you have just passed, corner of Twenty-sixth Street. At Twenty-fifth Street, Broadway, after intersecting the Fifth Avenue, by which the two form one broad highway for a couple of blocks, now sweeps

[*Madison Square—Fifth Avenue Hotel.*]

in its northerly course to the left, stretching quite to the extremity of the island.

Proceeding on the same side (right hand) of the way, the next white marble building is the Hoffman House, Broadway and Twenty-fifth Street. The Albemarle comes next, and the whole of the next block is occupied by the Fifth Avenue Hotel. Walk past this hotel, and cross the street to your left; you are now at the foot of Madison Square, and from this point you have a fine view of it and a part of Madison Avenue, the Worth House and Monument, while the classical proportions but simple architecture of the Fifth Avenue Hotel are presented to the greatest advantage.

Now stop the Wall Street omnibus, as before directed, going south or down town; seated in it you will pass, on your right, a succession of splendid buildings used—in fact built—expressly for retail stores by their present occupants. On the corner of Thirteenth Street and Broadway, at your left, is Wallack's Theatre. On your left, just above Tenth Street, is Grace Church, one of the most "fashionable" Espiscopal churches, and the next block, still on your left hand, is occupied by Stewart's Retail Store. Both are easily distinguished from other buildings. As you descend the city you pass many fine stores, the St. Denis, New York, the Grand Central, the Metropolitan, and St. Nicholas Hotels, and come to the "City Park," in which are situated the City Hall, the Court House and various Public Buildings for the city's use, and also the magnificent immense building, now in course of construction, for the United States Post Office and Court House. On reaching WALL STREET your omnibus will turn into it, and at this point you are *joined by the down-town traveller.*

Wall Street is a most striking street. Look at the buildings on both sides of it. Your omnibus will carry you to its terminus, the Wall Street Ferry. On arriving at the ferry you should cross the East River to Brooklyn, a few minutes' trip, and have a delightful water view and a breath of salt air.

Return with the boat, and reserve your tour of Brooklyn for a particular day. The same omnibus will take you to Broadway; and in the few moments you may have to wait for the stage, you will find abundance to interest you in the Cosmopolitan throng about the ferry, if you are an observer of human nature. But I would advise you *not* to take the omnibus. Walk back up Wall Street and observe closely, and at your leisure, the splendid buildings which American pride has erected for the most practical uses. You will easily distinguish the name and use of each one, flaunting in ambitious rivalry over its neighbor.

Pursue your walk to the corner of Wall and William Streets, where stands the U. S. Custom House, a mammoth granite building. Turn here to your *left*, and go down William Street a few steps, to its intersection with Beaver Street. There stands the traditional and time-honored restaurant, "DELMONICO." You will get nothing better to eat or to drink in the whole metropolis than here. Order an ice, if nothing more; but if it is lunch time, take it there. Then retrace your steps to the corner of Wall and William Streets, and walk up westerly to Broadway, observing all the buildings as you stroll along. On the corner of Nassau and Wall Street, at your right, is the UNITED STATES TREASURY, a conspicuous marble building with columns—perhaps the most solidly built structure in America. It was built for the Custom House, but transferred to the Treasury. Step in and examine the interior. In Broad Street, looking to the left, is the gilded pile built for and used as the STOCK EXCHANGE. Here you may be interested also, and if you are acquainted with a member, can find admittance into the stormy Babel within. As you approach Broadway, cast your eyes before you, and directly facing the head of Wall Street looms up in exquisite proportions the spire of TRINITY CATHEDRAL. It is one of the finest single spires in the world. Its *chimes* can scarcely be heard for the din in the streets. At the head of Wall Street turn down or to your left, and walk to the Bowling Green. Keep on as far as you can go, then turn to your right, and you will be at the BATTERY, the lowest extremity of the city. Observe and examine the more conspicuous buildings you may pass at this point. Stop here and breathe the air from the BAY. Around the Battery, and in a circuit of fifteen minutes' walk, is the *historical* part of the city, though there is nothing at present to indicate it, absorbed as it is by the vast and various practical enterprises peculiar to the spirit of the age, and eminently so of the American people—a spirit which defies even the illumination of recent heroic splendor, and forbids anything like a permanent atmosphere of romance or sentiment.

Many of the houses once occupied by the *élite* of the city are standing much as they were. They can be easily distinguished from other contiguous buildings by an indescribably private look. But the BATTERY, though considerably enlarged, is not greatly changed since that day. Here the refined, the lovely, the gay, were wont to display their charms in a morning or afternoon promenade; or, if more sentimentally inclined, stroll through its walks in small parties, and finish the evening in CASTLE GARDEN, in some pretty embowered arbor, enjoying their favorite ice-cream, not served in a saucer and shaped and tinted into artificial forms, but in high-piled tender-stemmed glasses, more suggestive of a commingling of classical associations than is the more material style of the present day. On the other hand, let humanity be grateful that the BATTERY is now a breathing spot for the humbler classes, to many of whom it is perhaps their only luxury; and that *Castle Garden*, now the *Emigrant Depot*, gives the poor wanderers to our hospitable shores a feeling of security they could not possibly know without it.

[*Castle Garden, at the Battery.*]

In its transition state, about twenty-five years ago, Castle Garden was used as a concert-hall, and here JENNY LIND made her first appearance in America.

From the Battery retrace your steps until you reach the Bowling Green again. Stop at the head of the Bowling Green, and wait for a Broadway and Fourth Avenue, or a Broadway and Twenty-third Street omnibus. Whichever you take, alight at Union Square, and linger a moment before you take another omnibus. Turn to page 40 for the most prominent objects from Wall Street to this point, reversing them, however, as you are now going *up*-town.

N.B.—It would be useless to give you at present the localities of any but such places as the most unaccustomed eye would instantly separate from their surroundings, because you do not yet know even the localities of the streets. You must have time to refer to your index and your map for particular directions. Enjoy, this first day, the inspiriting panorama! It will be the more vividly photographed upon your memory without those details which only confuse and harass the inexperienced sight-seer.

In the vicinity of Union Square, on your left, as you face the north, are many beautiful houses and private dwellings.;

but as Fashion creeps upward, most of them are hired by "fashionable boarding-house keepers," or are already in course of alteration for stores. In these boarding-houses many of the most respectable families choose to live,—preferring them, in some instances, to the hotels,—but transient boarders are not admitted.

At the southerly extremity of the square is what was several years ago a fashionable and expensive hotel, now converted into a theatre. Directly in front of it is an equestrian statue of Washington; opposite, on the Fourteenth Street side, is a statue of Lincoln. On the east side of the square runs Fourth Avenue. On the upper, or north side of the square is the "Everett House," and nearly opposite, corner of Fourth Avenue and Eighteenth Street, The Clarendon—both first-class hotels. Now, walk one block west to Fifth Avenue, step into a Broadway and Fifth Avenue omnibus, going north, and ride up to the Reservoir—a most beautiful specimen of masonry. Alight and ascend to its battlements, and walk around the embrasure, look into its two basins of water and at the surrounding streets. Descend and glance at the somewhat picturesque block facing the Reservoir, on Fifth Avenue. This is the *Rutgers Institute* and some private houses grouped together, producing a very pleasing effect. From hence walk easterly, and you are at Madison Avenue, and near the Grand Central Depot at Forty-second Street. Here commence the *walk* suggested at page   . After the walk, return to your hotel, dress, dine, and go to some place of amusement. (See Index for amusements, also the newspaper for that day.)

You have now, in *one day*, seen the exterior of what is most noteworthy in the metropolis. At your leisure you can, with the aid of the Handbook, pursue your investigations into the interior of the public, artistic, benevolent, mechanical, and trading life within it.

Your sight-seeing, so far, has been done without anxiety, hurry, or fatigue. It has been healthful recreation, not labor. You get home in ample time for the usual New York dinner hour at six, and at a moment when all that is interesting in the moving panorama without begins to fade from the streets; and with your spirits invigorated by the impressions of the day, you feel prepared for the very different diversions which the evening in the metropolis brings with it.

[Stock Exchange and U. S. Treasury—Corner Wall and Broad.]

SECOND DAY.

[*The Astor Library—Lafayette Place.*]

If Sunday, you have your choice of places of worship. (See Index.) The Sunday morning *Herald* also gives a list of many of the sermons to be preached on that day, and by whom and where.

If a week-day, after enjoying your breakfast and the morning paper, you will like to visit some of the public institutions— the Astor Library and the Cooper Institute, perhaps. (See Index.) If you are up-town, step to Madison Avenue, *east* from Broadway, and take a Madison Avenue omnibus. Tell the driver to stop with you at *Astor Place.* If you are at a down-town hotel, take any Broadway omnibus, and request the driver to drop you at *Astor Place.* Walk easterly one block and,

passing the Mercantile Library, you come to Lafayette Place—
a short street running southerly from Astor Place to Fourth
Street. On the west side of this short street is a row of buildings with columns, which formerly were *recherché* private residences. Opposite these, on the east side of the street, is the
Astor Library. The Cooper Institute, the Bible House, and
the Mercantile Library (originally built for an opera house), are
all grouped near here. (See Index.) You will find entertainment for a longer or shorter time, according to your feelings, at
these institutions. On leaving Astor Place, you may feel inclined
to take a walk; if so, stroll toward Second Avenue; you come to
it by walking easterly from any of the institutions you have been
visiting through Seventh or Eighth Streets. For many blocks
northward, this avenue is finely built up, and much of the
property is still owned and occupied by the descendents of the
old Dutch Governors. You may extend your walk in Second
Avenue as far up as *Stuyvesant Park*, stopping to visit the
rooms of the Historical Society, corner of Eleventh Street, or
you may prefer on reaching Fourteenth Street to walk through
it *westerly*, look at the Academy of Music, the New York Circus,
and Steinway Hall, and then walk up Irving Place to Gramercy
Park. Here you will see the Gramercy Park Hotel and the
Westminster, and walking along the upper side of the Park
westerly, the first street you reach is Lexington Avenue.
You have now seen the whole category of *fashionable* avenues.
Walk up Lexington Avenue a little way, and look at the Free
Academy—some day you may wish to enter it and see its
arrangements, and become acquainted with its plan. Turn
westerly from here and walk to Broadway. If you wish for
lunch, step into any confectionery, hotel, or restaurant near
you.

For the afternoon you will desire some variety of entertainment. The most enjoyable will be a drive to Central Park, indeed, every afternoon may be most agreeably and profitably devoted to this delightful recreation, and if it is any season but summer, you may spend your whole day from breakfast to dinner time out-doors to advantage, but in summer, beware of the heat in the middle of the day. At this season, in very warm days, at least four hours, from half-past eleven till half-past three should be spent in the repose of a shady room. Your drive to the Park should then be taken not earlier than four o'clock, and as it is the most delightful place you can be in on a summer afternoon, you can dine there (there is an admirable restaurant, see Index for Casino in Central Park), and return at evening in time for some place of amusement.

At any season except midsummer, return before dark.

We think the sight-seer may now be safely left with the "Handbook" to the guidance of the Index and Map and to his own inclinations and judgment.

He will speedily discover that our object in the preparation of this volume has been *not* to confuse and weary him by stale remarks and hackneyed observations about this or that, but to put him in a position to see, and admire, and criticize from his own stand-point of taste and opinion. We think the sight-seer requires ready hints, not stupid essays; and if we conduct him to a remarkable locality or a well-known structure, he will not care to have us stand perpetually at his elbow telling him what to admire, and what he ought not to be pleased with.

We suggest that in visiting institutions, it is a saving of time to take such ones for one day as are most nearly contiguous to each other, and to visit them in the morning, leaving the lighter objects of curiosity and interest to the after part of the day, when *recreation* will be more enjoyable than *research*. On visiting CENTRAL PARK, take *different* horse-cars on each visit, so as to enter by different approaches and have different views. You will see the whole Park in this way with less fatigue and less time, besides seeing in the various car-routes, through the streets, such of the metropolis as you might not otherwise be tempted to visit.

The principal Public Benevolent Institutions (see Index) are situated mainly in the suburbs of the city. They are imposing buildings, with carefully cultivated grounds, and in some instances command splendid views. These can all be visited by extending one of your drives in Central Park, if you go by private conveyance, while there are car routes which pass nearly all of them.

On taking leave of the sight-seer, let us assure him or her, of cheerful and welcoming looks wherever they may go, and an entire exemption from that system of *feeing* which is so harassing to the traveller in all parts of Europe. We must, notwithstanding, hint, that they should at all times and in all places, have a wary regard to the safety of all their personal property, including their *purses*, for in New York, as in all large places, there is a tendency among what would seem to be an irrepressible class to *fee themselves.*

AMUSEMENTS.

[*Booth's Theatre—Cor. Sixth Avenue and 23d Street.*]

BEFORE starting out for the day, it is prudent for those who desire to pass the evening at a place of amusement to secure seats in advance.

New York is distinguished for the number and variety of its recreations and amusements. The various peoples who gather here, including Germans, Irish, French, English, Swiss, etc., etc., and who have adopted the metropolis for their home, have, each in their way, established many of the amusements, sports, and games of their native land. While these are quite subordinate to the American element, they lend new and fresh features to the whole.

See daily morning papers "Amusement" column.

Operas and Theatres.

Places can be taken in advance at the Operas and Theatres with a choice of seats. Reserved seats are half a dollar more. Tickets can be got at the Offices in all the Theatres and Opera Houses. When a piece has a great run, it is best to secure seats some days in advance. These are reserved for the purchaser until after the first act of the play only.

Boxes must be taken entire; you cannot, as in Paris, take part of a box.

ACADEMY OF MUSIC—corner Irving Place and Fourteenth Street. First class. Private Boxes, full dress; Parquette, visiting cosume and dress bonnet; other parts of the house, walking suits.

AIMEE'S OPERA BOUFFE—720 Broadway.

BOOTH'S THEATRE—South-east corner of Sixth Avenue and Twenty-third Street. First class. Walking costume.

BOWERY THEATRE—46 Bowery.

BRYANT'S OPERA HOUSE—Negro Minstrels. West Twenty-third Street between Sixth and Seventh Avenues. First class. Walking costume.

CIRCUS—NEW YORK—Fourteenth Street nearly opposite Steinway Hall. (See "Steinway Hall.") First class. Walking costume.

FIFTH AVENUE THEATRE—Twenty-fourth Street, adjoining Fifth Avenue Hotel. First class. Walking costume.

FRENCH THEATRE—Fourteenth Street, north side, near Sixth Avenue. First class. Walking costume.

GRAND OPERA HOUSE—corner Eighth Avenue and Twenty-third Street, north-west side. First class. Private Boxes, full dress; Parquette, visiting costumes and dress bonnet; other parts of the house, walking suits.

NIBLO'S GARDEN—Broadway between Prince and Houston Streets, east side—lately destroyed by fire and rebuilding. First class people attend to see popular performances. Walking costume.

OLYMPIC THEATRE—624 Broadway. Amusing performances.

STADT THEATRE—German. 42 and 47 Bowery. First class. Walking costume.

ST. JAMES' THEATRE—corner Twenty-eighth Street and Broadway.

SAN FRANCISCO MINSTRELS—585 Broadway.

TONY PASTOR'S OPERA HOUSE—201 Bowery.

THEATRE COMIQUE—French. 514 Broadway.

UNION LEAGUE THEATRE—First class. *Private.*

UNION SQUARE THEATRE—corner of Fourteenth Street and Broadway.

WALLACK'S THEATRE—corner of Broadway and Thirteenth Street, north-west side. First class. Walking costume.

WOOD'S MUSEUM—Broadway, west side, near Thirty-first Street. Dress, walking costume.

PUBLIC BALLS.—These, in the winter, are a feature in New York of great variety in caste and class. They are fully advertised in the *Herald*, with all the necessary particulars. That called the "Charity Ball" is the most fashionable public ball of the season, and is especially patronized by the upper classes. It is always attended by foreign celebrities who happen to be in New York, and is gotten up with great splendor.

EGYPTIAN MUSEUM.—See "Historical Society."

STEINWAY HALL—Fourteenth Street, north side, between Irving Place and Fourth Avenue. First-class. Walking costume. Here are given lectures and concerts.

GERMAN MUSIC HALL—Adjoining Bowery Theatre. Every evening. Free. All classes, male and female, go; music, conversation, &c., &c.; Teutonic; respectable. It is quite an interesting incident to make the tour of these places along the Bowery, especially of a Saturday evening. The student of character has only to be provided with a sufficient quantity of small change to purchase a few glasses of lager—for no admission fee is demanded—and his visit will amply repay his expenditure of time and money. Here every phase of the German-American element is exhibited. Old and young, rich and poor, learned and ignorant, meet here in a motley but interesting group, upon perfect equality under the shadow of Gambrinus.

THOMAS'S CONCERTS—First-class. See daily newspapers for when and where they take place. Walking suits are worn to these. In summer they take place in Central Park.

In summer the German population are particularly fond of pic-nics, evening concerts in the open air, &c., &c., while target excursions, base-ball playing, boating, &c., &c., exist in great variety. In winter skating, curling, and sleigh-riding greatly abound.

PUBLIC LECTURES—Humorous lectures on current events, and on scientific, historical, and various popular subjects, are delivered during the winter season by different distinguished men, and are largely and fashionably attended. These are always advertised in the daily newspapers.

Art Galleries.

[*Academy of Design—East Twenty-third Street.*]

THE NATIONAL ACADEMY OF DESIGN—corner of Twenty-third Street and Fourth Avenue. Permanent Gallery of Paintings by American Artists. Admission 25 cents.

METROPOLITAN MUSEUM OF ART—Temporary Gallery, 681 Fifth Avenue. At last we have something to represent to us what the Louvre is to Paris and the National Gallery to London. To the vast body of the public who cannot afford to visit Europe the Metropolitan Museum of Art will supply a means of becoming acquainted with the works of the great artists of past ages. But the principal value of such a collection as has been brought together in Fifth Avenue is for the student, for he will be able now to study from his first step in art the manner of excellence of the different schools. About $130,000 has been expended on the collection. Preparations are being made to erect a suitable building for it in Central Park. The temporary gallery of the museum is open daily, except Sunday and Monday, from nine A. M. to five P. M., and on Monday evenings from seven to ten P. M. Admission to the public for the present is confined to Saturday, from 9 A. M. to 5½ A. M. On other days it is necessary to have tickets, which are placed at the disposal of all subscribers, but which can readily be obtained on written or personal application to the Honorary Superintendent, at the museum, or at his office, 54 East Twenty-third Street, or from any subscriber. The directors of this excellent institution are resolved not to allow any opportunity to pass in advancing the knowledge of art. Already several lectures have been given on various subjects connected with art, and the directory seem resolved to continue steadily in the road they have entered upon.

INSTITUTE OF FINE ARTS—625 Broadway. Paintings and Statuary.

AMERICAN MUSEUM OF NATURAL HISTORY—Central Park, Sixty-fourth Street and Fifth Avenue. Enter by Fifty-ninth Street entrance. The collection is large and valuable. On the first Tuesday of every month private receptions are given by the subscribers. On all other days the Museum is open to the public.

PRIVATE PICTURE GALLERIES.—These are far superior to anything on public exhibition, with the exception of the Metropolitan Museum of Art. The finest are the collections of John Taylor Johnston, William H. Aspinwall, August Belmont, Marshall O. Roberts, John Hoey, Robert L. Stuart, and Alexander T. Stewart. Applications should be made by letter, with your card enclosed. (See directory for residence.)

There are now residing in Rome between thirty and forty American painters and sculptors.

LEAVITT ART ROOMS—817 Broadway.
SOMEERVILLE ART GALLERY—82 Fifth Avenue.
SHAUS GALLERY—654 Broadway.
GOUPIL'S—corner Fifth Avenue and Twenty-Second Street. Beautiful paintings, engravings, and a thousand varieties of ornamental articles sold here. Also a picture gallery, open to the public *gratis*.

[*Cooper Institute—Fourth Avenue and Astor Place.*]

ASYLUMS.

[*Department of Public Charities—Third Avenue.*]

The benevolent institutions of the city are among its prominent features. New Yorkers are gay, mercurial, fond of pleasures and of fresh excitements, but in the midst of these, extraordinary attention has always been paid to the requirements of the unfortunate and to the situation of the numerous waifs, who may be termed the children of the metropolis, and who by desertion or from other cause have been left without natural protectors.

In addition, nearly every nationality is represented here by its appropriate society, which, while meeting for social purposes, is essentially a benevolent institution for the benefit of all who originally were of the same country.

ASYLUMS.

ASYLUM FOR AGED AND INFIRM SEAMEN—Sailor's Snug Harbor. (See "Benevolent Institutions.")

BLACKWELL'S ISLAND ASYLUMS—(See "Benevolent Institutions.")

BLIND ASYLUM—Ninth Avenue, between Thirty-third and Thirty-fourth Streets, occupying nearly three acres.

Well worth visiting to see the peculiar mode of instruction, which comprises all the ordinary branches of education. Open to visitors from 1 to 6 P.M., except Sunday.

[*Colored Orphan Asylum—Tenth Avenue.*]

COLORED ORPHAN ASYLUM—West One Hundred and Forty-third Street, Boulevard.

COLORED HOME—Sixty-fifth Street, near First Avenue.

ASYLUMS.

[*Deaf and Dumb Asylum—162d Street.*]

DEAF AND DUMB ASYLUM AT FANWOOD (Washington Heights)—One Hundred and Sixty-second Street. Take Hudson River Railroad. Exceedingly interesting to examine the ingenious methods of instruction. Can be visited every day between 1.30 and 4 o'clock.

GERMAN ORPHAN ASYLUM—Corner Avenue A and East Eighty-sixth Street.

HEBREW BENEVOLENT AND ORPHAN ASYLUM—East Seventy-seventh Street near Third Avenue.

INSANE ASYLUM—One Hundred and Seventeenth Street, west side of Tenth Avenue, Bloomingdale.

This is a branch of the New York Hospital; the grounds are large and fine, the buildings airy and capacious. The establishment admirably managed.

60 ASYLUMS.

[*Roman Catholic Orphan Asylum—Fifth Avenue.*]

ROMAN CATHOLIC ORPHAN ASYLUM—Fifth Avenue, between Fifty-first and Fifty-second Streets.

JUVENILE ASYLUM—For the protection and improvement of neglected children. Near High Bridge. See "High Bridge."

One of the most important charities of the city, retrieving from vagrancy and crime hundreds annually, and providing homes for them in the west. The grounds are large—over twenty acres—and are intended for the employment of the children.

Five hundred can readily be accommodated here, and two hundred in the "House of Reception" of this institution, at 71 West Thirteenth Street, open daily. Take Hudson River Railroad or Manhattanville Stages.

LYING-IN ASYLUM—*Charity.* 85 Marion Street. This institution, designed exclusively for married women, is in a most prosperous condition.

MAGDALEN ASYLUM—Eighty-eighth Street near Fifth Avenue.

ORPHAN ASYLUM—Beautifully located in grounds, comprising nine acres, near Eightieth Street, Bloomingdale. An old institution, well managed, accommodating over two hundred orphans. Open daily.

BENEVOLENT INSTITUTIONS.

BLACKWELL'S ISLAND.—East River.

Devoted Exclusively to the City Establishments.

Lunatic Asylum.
Almshouse and Hospital.
Penitentiary.
Hospital for Incurables.
New Work House for the purpose of separating mere vagrants from criminals; can accommodate six hundred people. Steamer foot of Twenty-seventh Street, East River, at 12 noon, also, ferry foot of Ninety-second Street and East River, at all hours.

[*House of Refuge—Randall's Island.*]

RANDALL'S ISLAND.—East River.

Devoted Exclusively to the City Establishments.

House of Refuge for the reformation of children.
Idiots' Hospital.
Infants' Hospital.
Steamer foot of Twenty-seventh Street, East River, at 12 noon, and ferry foot of Ninety-second Street and East River, cross at all hours. Take Second or Third Avenue Cars for ferry.

BENEVOLENT INSTITUTIONS. 63

These two islands and their institutions are of the most interesting character and are always visited by strangers.

PERMITS for visiting both islands are had of the "Department of Charities and Correction." See Index for "Departments."

WARD'S ISLAND.
Devoted Exclusively to the City Establishments.
Inebriate Asylum.
City Cemetery.
Ferry foot of One Hundred and Tenth Street, East River. Visitors should apply for admission to Commissioners of Emigration, New City Hall, in the Park. Same conveyance as to preceding Islands.

[*Sailor's Snug Harbor—Staten Island.*

SAILORS' SNUG HARBOR

For the maintainance and support of aged, decrepit, and worn-out sailors. Is situated at Port Richmond, Staten Island. Pier No. 19, North River, boats every hour except 1 P.M. Office of Trustees, 156 Broadway.

This noble charity was established in 1801 by Captain John Randall, who bestowed for its foundation a considerable quantity of land, then quite remote from New York, but now in the very heart of the city. By a systematic plan of leasing, these lands, which soon became city lots, now return a large and constantly increasing rental.

There is one hundred and sixty acres of land connected with the institution which accommodates three hundred old and disabled seamen.

SEAMAN'S FUND AND RETREAT.
HOME FOR SAILORS' CHILDREN.
MARINE HOSPITAL.

All at "Quarantine Grounds," Staten Island. Ferry Boats every hour from Whitehall Street.

BELLEVUE HOSPITAL.

Foot of Twenty-sixth Street, East River. Can be visited from 11 A.M. to 2 P.M.

BENEVOLENT SOCIETIES.

ARTISTS' FUND SOCIETY—Fourth Avenue, corner of East Twenty-third Street.
AMERICAN MUSICAL FUND SOCIETY—33 Delancey Street.
AMERICAN SEAMEN'S FUND SOCIETY—Office, 80 Wall Street.
AFRICAN SOCIETY FOR MUTUAL RELIEF—185 Bleecker Street

BENEVOLENT SOCIETIES.

ASSOCIATION FOR THE IMPROVED INSTRUCTION OF DEAF-MUTES—42 Seventh Avenue.

AMERICAN DRAMATIC FUND ASSOCIATION—842 Broadway. Open first Tuesday of every month.

ASSOCIATION FOR THE RELIEF OF RESPECTABLE INDIGENT FEMALES—226 East Twentieth Street.

AMERICAN HOME MISSIONARY SOCIETY—34 Bible House.

AMERICAN BOARD OF COMMISSIONERS FOR FOREIGN MISSIONS—31 Bible House.

COMMISSION OF HOME MISSIONS TO COLORED PEOPLE—57 Bible House.

[*Clinton Hall—Astor Place.*]

CHILDREN'S AID SOCIETY—11 Clinton Hall, Astor Place.

This institution is under no sectarian control, but is managed by a board of lady managers, representing all the Protestant denominations of the city, and by a like constituted board of gentlemen acting as trustees. Of course it is designed especially for the reception and nurture of foundlings and infants abandoned by impoverished or dissolute parents, and to aid in preventing the widespread and terrible crime of infanticide, as well as to give guidance and protection to the unfortunate mothers, and thus aid in saving them from destruction. At present there is no similar Protestant institution in New York, and, as a consequence, mothers with their children, representing every religious denomination, are compelled to enter the Asylum of the Roman Catholic sisters, or abandon their children, and thus let them become inmates of the Randall's Island Nursery, or finally place them in the care of some irresponsible person, in whose hands their lives are soon terminated by starvation and neglect. It is proposed to establish this Protestant asylum on the broadest basis. The results of the experience of the wisest physicians will be applied to the organization and operation of the charity. A country home, with all its salubrious surroundings, will be secured, and every precaution will be taken and every measure employed to carry out the beneficent intentions of the charter, and to render the New York Infant Asylum a praise even among the many noble charities of the metropolis.

COLORED RELIEF ASSOCIATION—No. 65 Bible House. [Servants provided for the South direct.]

COLONIZATION SOCIETY—New York, 42 Bible House.

FIVE POINTS HOUSE OF INDUSTRY—155 Worth Street.

FIVE POINTS MISSION HOUSE—Directly opposite.

Named Five Points from the circumstance of five streets meeting here at a point.

BENEVOLENT SOCIETIES. 67

Formerly the most disreputable spot in the city. Through the exertions, first of individuals, then of societies, it has become the seat of missions and is almost entirely reclaimed.

This charity is not sectarian. Visitors admitted daily, from 9 A.M. to 5 P.M.

FREEMASONS—Meet every evening corner of Broome and Crosby Streets, or at Odd Fellows' Hall, corner of Grand and Centre Streets.

The Masonic Temple, corner of Twenty-third Street and Sixth Avenue, will be completed within the year. The edifice is of granite, massive in construction, and very handsome. The top of the dome reaches 165 feet above the ground.

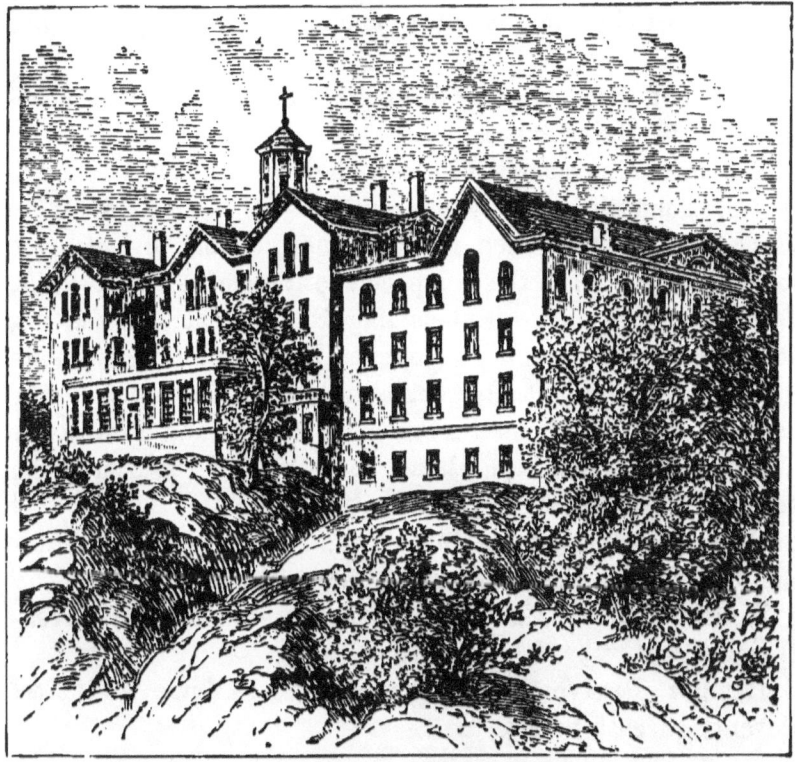

[Roman Catholic College—Boulevard & 131st Street.]

GERMAN BENEVOLENT SOCIETY—5 Battery Place.

GENERAL SOCIETY OF MECHANICS AND TRADESMEN—472 Broadway.

GERMAN MISSION HOUSE ASSOCIATION—426 Pearl Street.

HOWARD MISSION AND HOME FOR LITTLE WANDERERS—40 New Bowery. Open daily, from 8 A.M. to 5 P.M. Is not sectarian. Day school, musical exercises, church service, Sunday school, Sunday morning, breakfast.

The "little wanderers" of the Howard Mission are generously supplied with abundant gifts for their Christmas-trees. The principal booksellers of our city make large donations of books, others give toys, others cornucopias, while food and clothing are liberally donated, and the little people have a joyous time.

HELP FOR POOR GIRLS, OR YOUNG LADIES' CHRISTIAN ASSOCIATION—64 Irving Place.

The class of persons which it is desired principally to reach is not domestics, but young persons of education—those especially who have been reduced from comfort to a struggle for daily bread amid the sharp competition of New York life. Lonely and friendless girls—coming from the country, perhaps, to support aged parents or younger brothers and sisters—are most earnestly sought after, counselled, guided, and aided. The association is wholly non-sectarian, Catholics and Protestants alike being assisted, and already one-third of those applying to it have been placed in good positions.

HOME FOR FRIENDLESS, UNPROTECTED, AND DESTITUTE WOMEN AND CHILDREN—Office, 29 East Twenty-ninth Street.

HOME FOR AGED AND INFIRM ISRAELITES—215 West Seventeenth Street.

HEBREW BENEVOLENT SOCIETY—Third Avenue and East Seventy-seventh Street.

HIBERNIAN BENEVOLENT SOCIETY—195 West Seventeenth Street.

ITALIAN BENEVOLENT SOCIETY—685 Broadway.

IRISH EMIGRANT SOCIETY—51 Chambers Street.

LADIES' DEPOSITORY—876 Broadway.

This is an institution to give needle-work to reduced ladies and needy women at their own homes. The work is done in the best manner. Those who want work, and those who want work done, apply here.

MIDNIGHT MISSION FOR THE RESCUE OF FALLEN WOMEN—23 Amity Street, between Greene and Mercer Streets.

A most praiseworthy society, and already productive of great good.

NETHERLANDS EMIGRANT PROTECTIVE SOCIETY—224 William Street.

NEW ENGLAND SOCIETY—Astor House.

NEW YORK INFANTS' ASYLUM—24 Clinton Place.

ODD FELLOWS—Grand Lodge, corner Centre and Grand Streets.

PRESBYTERIAN HOME FOR AGED WOMEN—East Seventy-third Street, near Madison Avenue.

PROTESTANT EPISCOPAL SOCIETY FOR THE PROMOTION OF EVANGELICAL KNOWLEDGE—3 Bible House.

WILSON INDUSTRIAL MISSION—Corner of Eighth Street and Avenue A.

This institution was organized about nineteen years ago, and now embraces a day school, from 9 A.M. to 3 P.M., which is attended by two hundred girls, who are instructed in the elementary English branches, and, after a hearty dinner, are taught sewing by hand, while making their own garments, which they earn by a system of credit marks, thus securing them from the pauperizing influence of indiscriminate gratuitous distribution. There are also industrial classes of girls from twelve to twenty years of age, who are taught dressmaking and family sewing. This institution relies wholly for support on voluntary contributions. Its annual expenditures, with strict economy, amount to $9,000.

PORT SOCIETY FOR SEAMEN—72 Madison Street, corner of Catharine Street.

This embraces a church, mission station, temperance society, Sunday school, reading rooms, loan library, and bibles and miscellaneous books for circulation *gratis*.

ST. GEORGE'S SOCIETY—40 Exchange Place.

[*Seaman's Retreat—Staten Island.*]

SEAMEN'S FUND AND RETREAT—Office, 12 Old Slip; Quarantine, Staten Island.

SOCIETY FOR THE PREVENTION OF CRUELTY TO ANIMALS—Office, 696 Broadway.

Under the auspices of this society troughs for watering horses and thirsty dogs are placed at accessible spots all through the metropolis.

☞ For all other societies of all kinds see "City Register" in the New York Directory.

A ladies' association has been formed to promote the comfort of patients in the various charity institutions of the city. The widow of Admiral Farragut is President. A record is to be kept of the visits and the condition in which the inmates of the institution were found.

It is a noteworthy fact that the commissioners recently appointed to investigate the management of the organized charities in New York State received the keys of two hundred and forty charitable institutions.

CARS—(Street or Horse).

Their Starting Point, Terminus, and Route.

[*Depot of Third Avenue Horse Railroad.*]

CENTRAL PARK CARS.

Western or North River Division.—From South Ferry through Whitehall Street, to Battery Place, to West Street, to Tenth Avenue, to West Fifty-ninth Street, to Fifth Avenue (Central Park). Return by same route. Fare, each way, five cents.

Eastern or East River Division.—From South Ferry through Front Street, to Old Slip, to South Street, to Montgomery

Street, to South Street, to Jackson Street, to Monroe Street, to Grand Street, to Goerck Street, to East Houston Street, to Avenue D, to East Fourteenth Street, to Avenue A, to East Twenty-third Street, to First Avenue, to East Fifty-ninth Street, to Fifth Avenue. Return nearly same route. Fare, each way, five cents.

DRY-DOCK, EAST BROADWAY, AND BATTERY CARS.

From corner of East Fourteenth Street and Avenue B to East Eleventh Street, to Avenue D, to Eighth Street, to Lewis Street, to Grand Street, to East Broadway, to Chatham Street, to Park Row, to Ann Street. Returning same route to Columbia Street, and on to East Fourteenth Street.

SECOND AVENUE CARS.

From Peck Slip to Pearl Street, to Chatham Street, to Bowery, to Grand Street, to Allen Street, to First Avenue, to East Twenty-third Street, to Second Avenue, to Harlem, and return. Fare, five cents.

THIRD AVENUE CARS.

From Ann Street through Park Row to Chatham Street, to Bowery, to Third Avenue, to Harlem Bridge. Return the same route. Fare, five cents to East Sixty-fifth Street, six cents to East One Hundred and Thirtieth Street.

☞ There is a palace car on this line, fare fifteen cents.

FOURTH AVENUE CARS.

From Astor House through Centre Street to Grand Street, to Bowery, to Thirty-second Street.

Here one division turns East to Thirty-fourth Street Ferry and East River, and return.

The other division continues up Fourth Avenue to the Grand Central Depot (Forty-second Street), thence to Madison Avenue, up Madison Avenue to Central Park, and return. Fare to Thirty-fourth Street Ferry or Grand Central Depot, six cents; beyond that, eight cents.

[*Grand Central Depot—Forty-second Street.*]

GRAND CENTRAL DEPOT.

A new line of cars runs from the City Hall Park through Chatham Street, Bowery, and Lexington Avenue, to the Grand Central Depot. Passengers will find it more rapid and pleasant than by the Fourth Avenue line.

EIGHTH AVENUE CARS.

From corner Broadway and Vesey Street through Church Street, to Chambers Street, to West Broadway, to Canal Street, to Hudson Street, to Eighth Avenue, to West One Hundred and Twenty-fifth Street. Return by same route.

BROADWAY AND SEVENTH AVENUE, OR, AS THEY ARE SOMETIMES CALLED, UNIVERSITY PLACE CARS.

From Seventh Avenue to West Fifty-ninth Street, through Broadway to University Place, to Wooster Street, to West Broadway, to Barclay Street, to Broadway. Return through Barclay Street, to Church Street, to Greene Street, to Clinton Place, to University Place, to Broadway, to Seventh Avenue.

N.B.—Those marked "Seventh Avenue" turn off from University Place to Seventh Avenue; the others continue up Broadway to Seventh Avenue.

FORTY-SECOND AND GRAND STREET CARS.

From foot of West Forty-second Street to Tenth Avenue, to West Thirty-fourth Street, to Broadway, to East Twenty-third Street, to Fourth Avenue, to East Fourteenth Street, to Avenue A, to East Houston Street, to Grand Street, to Grand Street Ferry. Fare, five cents.

The general route is printed in large letters on outside of all cars.

For other City Railroad Routes see "City Register" in New York Directory. To be seen in all hotels, grocery stores, and apothecaries.

N.B.—The street cars run all night.

CLUBS.

[*Union League Club—Madison Avenue.*]

THE clubs of New York are well worth visiting. Among the most prominent may be mentioned the following:—

ARMY AND NAVY CLUB—The Army and Navy Club occupy the brown-stone building No. 8 West Twenty-eighth Street, between Broadway and Fifth Avenue. It has been elegantly fitted up as a club house. The club now numbers over two hundred members.

Century Club—No. 109 East Fifteenth Street. Composed of "Authors, Artists, and Amateurs." One of the most select clubs of the city.

Manhattan Club—No. 96 Fifth Avenue. The aristocratic Democratic (political) Club of New York.

New York Yacht Club is situated over the Jockey Club Rooms, on the corner of Twenty-seventh Street and Madison Avenue. These rooms are beautifully fitted up, and contain a perfect museum of nautical curiosities, comprising some handsome pictures, and a complete set of models of all the yachts that have belonged to the club. There are now over six hundred members to the club. The members have inaugurated a system of monthly dinners, which brings yachtsmen together and gives them an opportunity of talking over past and future yachting events. There is an annual cruise which is always fully advertised in detail in the daily papers.

Travellers' Club—No. 222 Fifth Avenue.

Union Club—No. 149 Fifth Avenue. Composed of old New Yorkers, and of rich bankers and brokers, and retired men of wealth.

Union League—Madison Avenue corner East Twenty-sixth Street. A very large, rich, and influential political (Republican) club (see illustration on page 76).

Clubs are only to be visited with a member, or by invitation on a member's application.

For other Clubs see "City Register," in New York Directory.

CHURCHES.

In Alphabetical Order.

Some of the most accessible of the principal churches of all denominations are:—

AFRICAN UNION—No. 161 West Fifteenth Street.

BAPTIST CHURCH — Corner of Thirty-first Street and Madison Avenue.

BETHEL—Colored—No. 214 Sullivan Street.

CONGREGATIONAL CHURCH—Corner Thirty-fourth Street and Sixth Avenue.

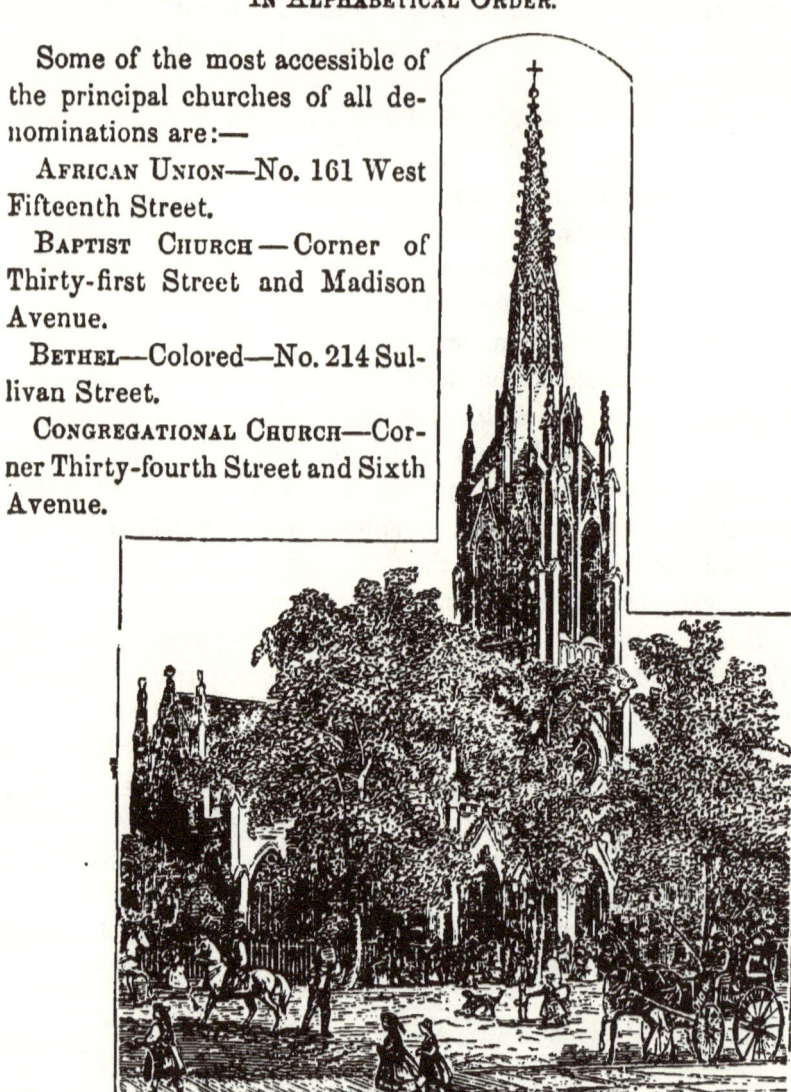

[*Grace Church—Broadway and Tenth Street.*]

CHURCHES.

CALVINISTIC CHURCH—225 East Thirteenth Street.

DUTCH REFORMED CHURCH—Corner Fifth Avenue and Twenty-ninth Street.

FRIENDS—East Twentieth Street, near Third Avenue.

FRENCH (PROTESTANT) CHURCH, named EGLISE DU ST. ESPRIT—Twenty-second Street, between Fifth and Sixth Avenues.

FRENCH ROMAN CATHOLIC CHURCH, named ST. FRANCIS XAVIER—No. 36 West Sixteenth Street.

GRACE CHURCH—(Episcopal). No. 800 Broadway, east side, near Tenth Street. Rev. Dr. Potter, Rector.

GERMAN EVANGELICAL REFORMED CHURCH—No. 97 Suffolk Street, east of Broadway.

GERMAN ROMAN CATHOLIC CHURCH, named CHURCH OF THE HOLY REDEEMER—Third Street, near Avenue A.

GERMAN LUTHERAN CHURCH—81 Christopher Street.

GREEK CHURCH (Russian)—No. 951 Second Avenue. Aside from the solemnity of the worship, which, claiming as it does to antedate all others, is interesting and inspiring from its antiquity, there is no more engaging entertainment than a visit to this chapel; and when the new church is completed it will probably be a popular resort, from the attractiveness of its Oriental architecture and the richness of its ceremonials.

JEWISH SYNAGOGUE—Corner Fifth Avenue and Forty-third Street. The visitor should not fail to see the interior.

LUTHERAN CHURCH—47 West Twenty-first Street.

METHODIST (Welsh).

METHODIST EPISCOPAL CHURCH, named ST. PAUL'S—Corner Fourth Avenue and Twenty-second Street.

MARINER'S CHURCH (Protestant)—Corner Madison and Catharine Streets.

PRESBYTERIAN CHURCH—Madison Avenue corner Twenty-fourth Street.

PRESBYTERIAN CHURCH—Corner Nineteenth Street and Fifth Avenue.

80 CHURCHES.

[*Jewish Synagogue—Fifth Avenue.*]

PRESBYTERIAN CHURCH (German)—290 Madison Street.

ROMAN CATHOLIC CHURCH, named ST. STEVEN's—149 East Twenty-eighth Street near Lexington Avenue.

The new magnificent Roman Catholic Cathedral is in Fifth Avenue, between Fifty-first and Fifty-second Streets.

RITUALISTIC CHURCH, named ST. ALBAN's—East Forty-seventh Street near Lexington Avenue.

ST. JOHN's—(Episcopal). In Varick Street. One of the ancient churches of the city. It has the grandest portico in the metropolis to-day; a work not surpassed in any of the London churches of the period in which it was built.

St. Paul's—(Episcopal). Broadway, between Vesey and Fulton Streets. In stately grace it still retains its proud place in ecclesiastical architecture. Here is a marble tablet to the memory of General Montgomery, also a monument to Thomas Addis Emmett.

Swedenborgian Church—114 East Thirty-fifth Street.

Trinity Church—(Episcopal, Cathedral). In Broadway directly facing Wall Street.

This church is open every day at all hours. In its graveyard is the tomb of Alexander Hamilton. From the steeple, which rises 334 feet from the ground, is a superb view of New York City and suburbs. It will amply repay the visitor to ascend it.

Trinity Chapel—A branch of Trinity Church. Is in East Twenty-fifth Street, near Broadway.

Unitarian Church, named Church of All Souls—Corner Fourth Avenue and Twentieth Street.

Universalist Church—Corner Fifth Avenue and Forty-third Street.

There are numerous "Bethels" for Sailors, along both the Hudson and East Rivers.

N.B.—For all other churches, of which there is in New York a very great number and variety, see "City Register," end of New York Directory.

Directory to be seen at Hotels. Groceries, and Apothecaries.

COMPANIES.

[*Knickerbocker Life Insurance Co.—Broadway, cor. Park Row.*]

COMPANIES. 83

No attempt is made to give a list of the numerous business companies of the city. Many of these occupy superb buildings (see illustrations), but only those are mentioned which by possibility the traveller may desire to have access to.

AMERICAN EMIGRANT COMPANY—4 Bowling Green.
ADAMS EXPRESS COMPANY—59 Broadway.
ATLANTIC COAST MAIL STEAMSHIP COMPANY—187 West Street.
ATLANTIC MAIL STEAMSHIP COMPANY—5 Bowling Green.
AMERICAN MERCHANTS' UNION EXPRESS—115 Broadway.
ANCHOR LINE OF STEAMSHIPS—7 Bowling Green.
BANKERS AND BROKERS' ASSOCIATION—25 Broad Street.
CENTRAL AMERICAN TRANSIT COMPANY—56 Exchange Place.
CUNARD LINE MAIL STEAMSHIP COMPANY—111 Broadway.
HAMBURG-AMERICAN PACKET COMPANY—61 Broadway.
INMAN LINE STEAMSHIP COMPANY—15 Broadway.
KNICKERBOCKER LIFE INSURANCE CO.—239 Broadway. (*See cut, page* 82.)
NORTH GERMAN LLOYD STEAMSHIP COMPANY—New York, Southampton, and Bremen. Office, 2 Bowling Green.
NEW YORK ASSOCIATED PRESS—83 Liberty Street.
NATIONAL EXPRESS COMPANY—65 Broadway.
NATIONAL LINE OF STEAMSHIPS—New York and Liverpool, and New York and London. Office, 69 Broadway.
PACIFIC MAIL STEAMSHIP COMPANY—59 Wall Street.
SAFE DEPOSIT COMPANY—146 Broadway.
TELEGRAPHY.—*American Telegraph Company, Western Union.*—The head-quarters of this Company are corner of Broadway and Liberty Street. It has a capital of over $2,000,000, employs over 20,000 miles of wire, has 800 officers, and the names of 2,000 on its pay-roll. Its expenses are over half a million of dollars a year.
TRANSATLANTIC MAIL STEAMSHIP COMPANY—58 Broadway.
UNITED STATES EXPRESS COMPANY—82 Broadway.

84 COMPANIES.

[*Gilsey House—Broadway, cor. 29th street.*]

UNITED STATES MAIL LINE OF STEAMSHIPS—29 Broadway.
WESTCOTT'S EXPRESS COMPANY—785 Broadway.
WHITE STAR LINE OF STEAMSHIPS—19 Broadway.

CONSULS.

Austria—33 Broadway.
Belgium—45 Worth Street.
Brazil—13 Broadway.
Baden—68 Broad Street.
Bavaria—85 Nassau Street.
Bolivia—63 Pine Street.
Chili—249 West Forty-second Street.
Colombia—25 William Street.
Costa Rica—19 Broad Street.
Denmark—112 Front Street.
Dominica—23 William Street.
Ecuador—7 Broadway.
France—4 Bowling Green.
Great Britain—17 Broadway.
Greece—47 Exchange Place.
Guatemala—13 South William Street.
Hayti—29 Front Street.
Hawaiian Islands—24 Beaver Street.
Hesse-Darmstadt—58 Beaver Street.
Honduras—135 East Thirty-ninth Street.
Italy—7 Broadway.
Liberia—42 Bible House.
Mexico—52 Exchange Place.
Monaco—4 Bowling Green.
Netherlands—45 Exchange Place.
Norway—18 Exchange Place.
Nicaragua—
North German Union—117 Broadway.
Peru—26½ Broadway.

Portugal—148 Pearl Street.
Paraguay—91 Wall Street.
Russia—25 Old Slip.
Spain—29 Broadway.
Sweden—18 Exchange Place.
Switzerland—23 John Street.
Turkey—66 Broadway.
Uruguay—19 Broad Street.
Venezuela—121 Front Street.

Fire Department, Head Quarters—127 Mercer Street.]

DEPARTMENTS.

[*Old Post Office—Corner Nassau and Cedar Streets.*]

CORONERS' OFFICE—11 City Hall.

COMMISSIONERS OF EMIGRATION—Office, Castle Garden.

COMMISSIONERS OF CHARITIES AND CORRECTION—Corner East Eleventh Street and Third Avenue.

COMMISSIONERS OF EDUCATION—Corner Grand and Elm Streets.

EXCISE DEPARTMENT.—299 Mulberry Street.

FREE LABOR BUREAU.—8 Clinton Place.

HEALTH DEPARTMENT—301 Mott Street.
LAW DEPARTMENT—82 Nassau Street.
MARINE COURT—32 Chambers Street.
MAYOR'S OFFICE—City Hall, No. 6, first floor.
MILITARY PAY DEPARTMENT—Corner Greene and West Houston Streets.
OLD POST OFFICE.—Nassau Street, between Cedar and Liberty Streets (see illustration on page 87).
PORT WARDEN—Office, 52 South Street; open 7 A.M. to 5 P.M.
PUBLIC PARKS—Office, 265 Broadway.
POLICE PROTECTIVE AND DETECTIVE DEPARTMENT—Central Depot, 300 Mulberry Street.
POLICE TELEGRAPH—
This proves to be a very successful mode of detecting crime.
PUBLIC ADMINISTRATOR—Office, 115 Nassau Street.
DEPARTMENT OF PUBLIC INSTRUCTION—Corner Grand and Elm Streets.
DEPARTMENT OF PUBLIC WORKS—Office, 237 Broadway.
POLICE COURTS—
  At the Tombs, corner Centre and Franklin Streets.
  At City Hall.
  At East Fifty-seventh Street.
  At 69 Essex Street.
SCHOOL COMMISSIONERS' OFFICES—
  665 Broadway.
  237 Broadway.
  285 Broadway.
  Herald Building, Corner Ann Street and Broadway.
  54 Wall Street.
  785 Beekman Street.
UNITED STATES ASSAY OFFICE—30 Wall Street. Visitors admitted from 11 to 12 A.M. No deposits received of less than $100.
UNITED STATES NAVY PAYMASTER—29 Broadway.

EXCURSIONS.

[*Blackwell's Island—East River.*]

BY all means visit the larger Institutions situated on the various Islands in the East River.

There are also delightful drives in all directions from the Metropolis: beyond Central Park into Westchester County, on both the North River and East River sides:—across the different Ferries into New Jersey; also to Staten Island and Long Island; much lovely scenery and many beautiful villages can be seen, by taking a carriage for the day, and driving leisurely in any direction, stopping to lunch and rest your horses when and where you feel inclined.

The North and East River steamboats are a delightful mode of taking excursions.—See Steamboat Travel in Index. The "Excursion Boats" are usually monopolized by the middle and lower classes, especially on Sunday. Sunday excursions of any kind, are not considered in good taste in New York, except among the foreign population. There is quite enough to interest a stranger in the city on the fashionable avenues, at church, and in visiting charitable institutions, to keep him well employed within the Metropolis.

Many places in the environs of New York can readily be visited by steam-cars and horse-cars, but we advise the stranger to avoid these modes of conveyance whenever he can, as the charm of these short excursions consists of the drive or sail, although, if expense has to be considered, the horse-cars are by far the cheapest means of conveyance.

A trip on the Hudson should be a matter of course with the traveller. No one would visit New York without passing up or down this perhaps most beautiful river in the world. Though it does not possess the castellated fortresses and historical associations which have made the Rhine so celebrated, it surpasses its far-famed rival in grand and never-ending scenes and in a wealth and beauty of landscape. To view it to advantage, go by boat. The steamboats themselves are worth seeing; they are floating palaces.

EAST RIVER.—Blackwell's Island and Randall's Island, containing Prisons, Small-pox Hospitals, Lunatic Asylums, Houses of Refuge for children, etc.

HUDSON RIVER.—For trip up the Hudson take morning boat, Pier 39 North River, foot of Vesey Street. See "Steamboat Travel" in index. Most noteworthy points on the Hudson are,—

FORT WASHINGTON.

THE PALISADES.

SUNNY SIDE—Residence of Washington Irving.

TAPPAN—Headquarters of Washington, and place of André's execution.

TARRYTOWN—Place where André was captured.

SEEEPY HOLLOW—Scene of Irving's "Legend of Sleepy Hollow."

SING SING—State's Prison.

Stony Point—Site of old Fort.
West Point and the Highlands—Military Academy.
Idlewild—Residence of the late N. P. Willis, the poet.
Fishkill—Grand scenery.
Newberg—Headquarters of Washington.
Catskill Mountains.
These places can also be visited separately by rail.

Places on west shore of the Hudson by Erie Railroad, and on the east shore by the Hudson River Railroad.

We have not undertaken to give any "guide" to the Hudson River, only some prominent points of special interest. The traveller will find everywhere on sale picturesque maps of the river, with notes and descriptions.

[Columbia College—Fiftieth Street.]

FERRIES.

[*Brooklyn Ferry House—Fulton Street.*]

FOR many years about the year 1644, there lived an industrious, hard-working Hollander near what is now Peck Slip, who, finding that persons occasionally desired to cross the East River, undertook to ferry over foot passengers in a little skiff, for a small sum payable in wampum. As he could not afford to "watch and wait" for customers, he suspended a large tin horn to a branch of a tree near the river, on which the traveller was forced to practise till the ferryman was summoned.

In the year 1655 a more elaborate arrangement was made, a

ferry ordinance having been passed by the officials of New Amsterdam. Ferry-houses were built, and rates established by law. After 1667, when the rights and privileges of a town were confirmed by patent upon Brooklyn, the establishment of ferries became a bone of contention between New York and Brooklyn, which served for both sides of the river to pick at for something like a hundred years. Just before the Revolutionary war three regular ferries were established.

TO BROOKLYN.

FULTON FERRY, foot of Fulton street, to Fulton street in Brooklyn.

From 3 A.M. to 12 P.M. every 10 minutes. From 12 to 3 A.M. every 15 minutes.

Fulton street, Brooklyn, is a thoroughfare and mart.

Fulton street runs out of Broadway *easterly*. Take Broadway and Fifth Avenue omnibus.

HAMILTON AVENUE FERRY, foot Whitehall street, New York, to Atlantic Dock, Brooklyn. Boats cross from 7 A.M. to $6\frac{1}{2}$ P.M. every 10 minutes. From $6\frac{1}{2}$ to 9 P.M. every 15 minutes. From 9 P.M. to 7 A.M. every half-hour.

SOUTH or ATLANTIC FERRY, foot of Whitehall street to Atlantic street in Brooklyn.

From 5 A.M. to 11 P.M. every 12 minutes. From 11 P.M. to 5 A.M. every half hour.

Whitehall street is at the lower *easterly* extremity of the city. Take Broadway and Fourth Avenue or 23d street omnibus.

WALL STREET FERRY, foot of Wall street, to Montague street in Brooklyn.

From 5 A.M. to 8 P.M. every 10 minutes. From 8 P.M. to midnight every 20 minutes.

Montague street, Brooklyn, is a private and beautiful street.

This is the "Court end" of that city.

Wall street runs out of Broadway *easterly*. Take Madison avenue omnibus.

WILLIAMSBURG—or BROOKLYN, E. D., Ferry foot of East Houston street, New York, to Grand street, in Brooklyn, E. D., and Ferry foot of Grand street, New York, to Grand and South 7th streets in Brooklyn, E. D. 42d and Grand street cars will take you to these ferries.

STATEN ISLAND.

For Hoboken, New Jersey, foot of Barclay street, North River. Barclay street runs out of Broadway *westerly*. Take Broadway and 7th Avenue cars.

Also for Hoboken, foot of Christopher street, from 5 A.M. to 8 P.M. every 15 minutes. From 8 to 12 P.M. every 20 minutes.

For New Brighton, Sailor's Snug Harbor, Castleton, Fort Richmond, and Elm Park. PIER 19, North River. Boats go every hour except 1 P.M.

For Philadelphia, Baltimore, and Washington, Jersey City Ferry foot of Cortlandt street, North River.

For Tompkinsville, Stapleton, and Vanderbilt's Landing, foot of Whitehall street, from 6 A.M. to 9 P.M. every hour.

Also at 11:45 P.M. the 6, 7, and 9 A.M. and 1, 4, 5 and 6 P.M. boats connect with the TRAINS of the Staten Island Railroads. Take Broadway and Fourth Avenue or 23d street omnibus.

For all other Ferries and for Piers, see "City Register" in New York Directory. To be seen in every Hotel, Grocery Store, or Apothecary.

FORTS.

[*Fort Richmond—Staten Island.*]

AIR weather and pleasant excursions may be enjoyed, by visiting the Fortifications on the neighboring Islands.

FORT HAMILTON—Long Island—The Narrows. Horse Railroad from Brooklyn to Fort Hamilton; also Steamboat.

An elaborate work with all modern war contrivances.

FORT LA FAYETTE—The Narrows.

An island fort—now almost a ruin—of no use as a defence. Famous for being the place of confinement for prominent political prisoners during our civil war.

FORT TOMPKINS—Staten Island—The Narrows.

A formidable fortification admirably constructed.

Fort Richmond—Staten Island—The Narrows.

A dangerous "work" for an enemy.

The "Narrows" are so called because here the Long Island and Staten Island shores, after forming the magnificent "Lower Bay," suddenly contract to within a distance of about four-fifths of a mile of each other. Here the land is high, and here a series of menacing forts guard the approach to the city. This passed, the shores again recede, forming the Upper Bay.

Fort Columbus and Castle William—Governor's Island, facing Castle Garden.

These two fortifications have underground connection and are for the defence of the inner harbor. Castle William especially is an important work 600 feet in circumference and 60 feet high. At Fort Columbus is stationed a corps of United States soldiers.

Of easy access by rowboat from Castle Garden—Battery.

There are also important fortifications on Bedlow's Island and Ellis Island—two small Islands in the upper Bay lying nearly opposite, west, to Governor's Island.

Other fortifications near Sandy Hook and to guard Long Island Sound are not mentioned.

The Fort Hamilton and Coney Island, and also the Long Branch steamers give you a view of these Forts. For these steamers see index for "Summer Resorts."

HACKNEY COACHES, HACKMEN, CARRIAGES AND CABS.

The rates for "hacks" in New York are exorbitant compared with those of any other city, and the drivers are often unscrupulous and extortionate. It is always best, therefore, for the stranger to arrange in advance what he is to pay for the desired service, and with the "Hand-book" before him he will know exactly what that should be.

Whenever the sight-seer can use an omnibus or street car let him do so and avoid the hacks. If he is staying at a hotel we advise him to order a carriage for driving out at the office.

RATES.

One passenger, one mile or less....................	50
Each additional passenger........................	37½
One passenger, any distance within two miles.......	75
Every additional passenger	37½
For one passenger to new ALMS HOUSE, and return..	$1 00
Each additional passenger...	50
To HARLEM (one or more passengers, and return), to remain three hours or less..................	5 00
To the HIGH BRIDGE one or more passengers, and return, to remain three hours or less...............	5 00
To KING'S BRIDGE (for one or more passengers, and return), to remain all day or less time............	5 00
For use of hackney coach or carriage, by the day, for one or more passengers.........................	5 00
For the use of hackney coach or carriage, by the hour, to stop when and where as often as you please.....	1 00

For infants no charge.
For children under 14 years, half price.

In case of disagreement as to price the matter may be laid before the Mayor.

Fastidious persons will prefer to go to a first-class livery stable, or first-class hotel, for a more elegant equipage, though at a higher price. There is no danger of extortion at these. Charges are $2 an hour, and for a party, opera, or theatre, to go and return, from $3 to $4.

[*Rutgers Female College—Fifth Avenue.*]

HOTELS.

Among the prominent hotels in the Metropolis are the

ASTOR HOUSE—Broadway, between Barclay and Vesey streets. European plan. First class. Cars start every few moments for up town from the Astor. This is the most eligible, first class hotel for business and commercial men who wish to stop down town. It ranks with the Queen's Hotel, St. Martins-le-Grand, and the Old London Coffee House, London.

[*Fifth Avenue, corner of 26th street—Hotel Brunswick.*]

N.B.—There are several very respectable *Second Class* Hotels in Cortlandt street, near Broadway, including the " Western," the "Merchants," the "National," etc., well adapted to the wants of business men who desire to stop down town, and who wish to consult economy.

ASHLAND HOUSE—European plan, corner Fourth avenue and 24th street. Second class. Rooms and meals reasonable.

BREVOORT HOUSE—Corner Fifth avenue and Eighth street. European plan. First class.

CLARENDON HOTEL—Corner Fourth avenue and 18th street. American plan. First class.

FIFTH AVENUE HOTEL—Fifth avenue, 23d, and 24th streets. American plan. First class.

[*The Grand Hotel—Broadway, corner of 31st street.*]

HOTELS.

GRAND HOTEL—Corner 31st street and Broadway. European plan. First class.

The Fifth Avenue Hotel and the Grand Hotel, are eligible first-class houses for the sight-seer. They are each probably the best type of their kind in the country, the Fifth Avenue being a very perfect exposition of the purely American style of hotel-life, and the Grand the most finished in its details on the European plan. They are also perhaps the most expensive.

HOTEL BRUNSWICK—Madison Square, corner of Fifth avenue and 26th street—European Plan, First class. N.B.—Café on first floor.

HOFFMAN HOUSE—Corner of Broadway and 25th street. European plan. First class.

NEW YORK HOTEL—Broadway, Washington place and Waverley place. First class. Much frequented by Southerners.

PUTNAM COUNTY HOUSE—Corner 26th street and Fourth avenue. European plan. Third class. Strictly respectable.

Rooms and clean beds from 50 cents to 75 cents per day.

It is largely frequented by drovers, milkmen, and marketmen generally. It is open all night, and hot meals of excellent quality are served at all hours of the night as well as day, and at very moderate charges. It is curious to look in at one, two, or three o'clock in the morning to see who are customers at such hours for hot steaks and hot cakes and coffee.

There are a large number of first, second, and third class hotels scattered through the city of the highest respectability. We by no means undertake to give a list of all.

At all hotels on the European plan, meals can be got at any hour between 7 o'clock in the morning and 12 o'clock at night.

LITERARY AND SCIENTIFIC INSTITUTIONS.

AMERICAN GEOGRAPHICAL AND STATISTICAL SOCIETY—Cooper Institute. Open to members and to others on invitation.

AMERICAN INSTITUTE—Cooper Institute, Agricultural and Mechanical. Open to members and invited guests.

The first "Great Medal of Honor" ever awarded by the American Institute to an inventor of that association was recently presented to Mr. James Lyall, inventor of the "Positive-motion Loom." This invention has been applied, with great success, to the weaving of cloths of all kinds, performing much more work in the same time than is possible by the old processes. This medal was awarded in 1869.

APPRENTICES' LIBRARY—In Mechanics' Hall, 472 Broadway, near Grand street. Open to members.

ANTHROPOLOGICAL INSTITUTE—Formerly the Ethnological Society, corner Second avenue and East 11th street. Open to members and invited guests.

This Society publishes the "Journal of the Anthropological Institute of New York." In the late change the scope of the society has been greatly enlarged, and many of the difficulties attendant upon the maintenance of the old organization have been obviated. There is little doubt that the new society will occupy a prominent place in advancing knowledge in the world.

ASTOR LIBRARY, east side Lafayette place, near Astor place. Founded by John Jacob Astor.

Containing over one hundred thousand volumes, full of literary treasures.

Open to the public from 10 A.M. to 5 P.M.

The sight-seer must not omit to visit this library.

AMERICAN MICROSCOPICAL SOCIETY, 64 Madison avenue.

LITERARY AND SCIENTIFIC INSTITUTIONS.

BIBLE HOUSE—Astor place.—Astor place is a street of but two blocks, running out of Broadway, east side, a block below Eighth street.

[*Bible House—Fourth Avenue and Astor Place.*]

The Bible House fronts on Fourth avenue, Astor place, and Third avenue. It is a gigantic building of brick, with stone facings. The principal entrance is on Fourth avenue.

It has put in circulation over 10,000,000 of Bibles and Testaments, and produces them in various dialects. A large number of benevolent societies and missions have their offices in this building.

CITY LIBRARY—12 City Hall—open to the public daily, from 10 to 4 o'clock.

COLUMBIA COLLEGE—Forty-ninth street, between Fourth and Fifth avenues.

An old and famous seminary of learning.

CLINTON HALL—Formerly Astor Place Opera House.—Astor place. (*See illustration, page 65.*)

This is the first structure ever erected solely for Opera in New York. On an attempt to render it exclusive—one of the regulations being that no one could obtain a seat unless in full dress with white gloves—the house became exceedingly unpopular with the lower classes, and fashionable people were actually pelted with snowballs as they were entering. This feeling was not the ostensible though probably the real cause of the famous Macready riot, for the populace gladly availed themselves of the feeling manifested by "Upper Tendom" toward their favorite actor Forrest, and undertook to stop the performances of Macready by force. The military were called out and were obliged to fire on the mob, killing several before they could disperse it. This, while the law was properly vindicated, threw a shadow over the spot as a place of amusement, and it was finally sold for other purposes.

We may add that the absurd attempt at anti-republican customs, even in small things, was effectually cut short.

CONVENT OF THE SACRED HEART—Manhattanville—a short drive from Central Park. Fine and extensive building and grounds.

COOPER UNION—Fronts on Seventh and Eighth streets and on Third and Fourth avenues.

Founded by Peter Cooper. Contains an art gallery for students in art, free, a large library, lecture-rooms, school of design for women, &c., &c., &c.

FREE ACADEMY—or College of the City of New York—Corner Lexington avenue and Twenty-third street.

LITERARY AND SCIENTIFIC INSTITUTIONS.   105

This College is for rich and poor. The best classical education can be obtained here. All the expenses, including instruction, are paid out of the public treasury. A high order of scholarship prevails.

GENEALOGICAL AND BIOGRAPHICAL SOCIETY—Open to members and invited guests—64 Madison avenue.

[*Egyptian Museum—Interior of Historical Society.*]

HISTORICAL SOCIETY—Open to members and invited guests—Corner Second avenue and Eleventh street. Egyptian Museum.

LADIES' ART ASSOCIATION—20 Clinton Hall, Astor place.

LYCEUM NATURAL HISTORY—Fourteenth street near Fourth avenue. Open to the public.

MERCANTILE LIBRARY—Clinton Hall, Astor place. Visitors admitted. (*See illustration, page* 65.)

Originally for merchants' clerks. The public admitted to the privileges of the reading-room and library for $5 per annum. The largest collection of books in the city except the Astor Library.

MECHANICS' INSTITUTE—20 Fourth avenue. Open to members. Large library.

MECHANICS' SOCIETY SCHOOL—General Society of Mechanics and Tradesmen. Society's building, 472 Broadway. The society is one of the oldest organizations in the United States, having been instituted in 1798 and incorporated in 1820. Eighteen years ago the evening school was opened. It has been continued with success ever since. At present it contains 430 pupils, mostly the sons of mechanics and themselves apprentices to some mechanical trade. Bookkeeping, writing, and drawing are taught. This institution is free. There are three freehand classes in the school, one for mechanical and one for architectural drawing. The school is under the management of a committee of twelve members of the society.

MOTT MEMORIAL—Free Medical Library—64 Madison avenue. Open to the public.

NATIONAL ACADEMY OF DESIGN—Corner of Twenty-third street and Fourth avenue. Instituted in 1826. Annual exhibitions in May, June and July. Works of living artists only. Admission 25 cents. (*See illustration, page* 54.)

The National Academy of Design has resolved to open an exhibition of that institute on Sundays to the people, from 12 M. to 6 P. M., at a reduction of the entrance fee to 15 cents.

Samuel Morse, the father of telegraphy, was also the founder of the National Academy of Design. It was at first a mere

LITERARY AND SCIENTIFIC INSTITUTIONS. 107

drawing association, organized by himself and a few other artists, in 1824. After it became an academy Mr. Morse was its first President, and continued in office sixteen years.

NEW YORK LAW INSTITUTE—41 Chambers street, Law Library, open daily to members.

NEW YORK UNIVERSITY—Washington square, east side.

NEW YORK CONSERVATORY OF MUSIC—820 Broadway.

[*Society Library—University Place.*]

NEW YORK SOCIETY LIBRARY—University place, near 12th street. Founded in 1754, contains 40,000 volumes, visitors admitted.

POLYTECHNIC ASSOCIATION OF THE AMERICAN INSTITUTE—24 Cooper Institute.

PRINTERS' FREE LIBRARY—3 Chambers street, open Saturday evenings.

SCHOOL OF ART—Cooper Institute.

THEOLOGICAL SEMINARY—corner Twentieth street and Ninth avenue.

UNION THEOLOGICAL SEMINARY—9 University place.

WOMAN'S LIBRARY—in New York University Building.

YOUNG MEN'S CHRISTIAN ASSOCIATION—corner Fourth avenue and Twenty-third street, visitors admitted. It contains Reception-room, bathing-room, bowling alley, gymnasium, class-rooms, library, lecture-room, parlor, reading-room, and lecture hall.

The building and lots cost five hundred thousand dollars, three hundred and fifty thousand dollars of which was given to the Association for the purpose by the merchants interested in the work. This is one of the most praiseworthy and best managed institutions in the city. It was organized in 1852. It was especially intended for young men who come from the country to enter in business life here. The idea was to present to such, and indeed to all young men, so agreeable a spot to spend their evenings in that they would irresistibly be drawn to it. This has proved an entire success.

The building is elegantly furnished, and presents a cheering appearance during the long winter evenings. Open fires of soft coal blaze in every room, and crowds of young men can be seen in every room with happy faces. Any young man is welcome, be he member or not.

There are classes for French, German, Book-keeping, Writing, Gymnastics, and a Glee Club.

A ticket costing five dollars admits the owner to all the above classes, and to the use of gymnasium, bowling-alley, and baths for one year.

LITERARY AND SCIENTIFIC INSTITUTIONS. 109

Besides the buildings above described, the Association contains three branches, viz.: at 285 Hudson street—at 473 Grand street—and at 125th street, between Third and Fourth avenues.

[*Historical Society—Second Avenue.*]

MEDICAL INSTITUTIONS.

[*Harlem Dispensary—Fourth av. and 125th Street.*]

COLLEGE OF PHYSICIANS AND SURGEONS—Corner of 23d street and Fourth avenue. Founded in 1807. The college has a corps of eight professors and is well attended. For admittance to the Museum apply to the Janitor.

COLLEGE OF DENTISTRY—Corner Broadway and East 21st street.

COLLEGE OF FEMALE PHYSICIANS—Corner Second avenue and 12th street.

MEDICAL INSTITUTIONS.

COLLEGE OF PHARMACY—No 90 East 13th street.

HOMŒOPATHIC MEDICAL COLLEGE—Third avenue and East 20th street.

MEDICAL COLLEGE AND CHARITY HOSPITAL—In the City Hospital, 319 Broadway, rear of the lot.

NEW YORK MEDICAL COLLEGE—No. 90 East 13th street. Founded in 1850. Valuable museum, laboratory, etc. Able corps of professors.

DISPENSARY AND HOSPITAL OF THE WOMEN'S INSTITUTE—459 Sixth avenue. Lady Physician in charge.

DISPENSARY FOR THROAT AND CHEST DISEASES—234 Fifth street. Open Mondays, Wednesdays, and Fridays, from 1 to 3 P.M.

DEMILT DISPENSARY—401 Second avenue. Medical attendance from 9 A.M. to 4 P.M. Open daily. Sundays from 9 to 10 A.M. and from 1 to 2 P.M.

EASTERN DISPENSARY—57 Essex street, corner of Grand street. Open from 8 to 6 for medicine. Medical attendance 9 to 3.

GERMAN DISPENSARY—No. 8 Third street. Open daily, except Sundays, from 1 to 5 P.M.

HOMŒOPATHIC DISPENSARY—493 Seventh avenue. Open daily, except Sundays, from 11 A.M. to 3 P.M.

MANHATTAN DISPENSARY—Corner 131st street and Tenth avenue.

NEW YORK HOMŒOPATHIC DISPENSARY—109 West 34th street. Open from 10 to 4.

NEW YORK CITY DISPENSARY—114 White street, corner Centre street. Open daily, except Sundays and holidays, from 9 A.M. to 5 P.M. for medicine. For medical attendance 10 A.M. to 3 P.M., Sundays from 9 to 10 A.M.

NORTH EASTERN DISPENSARY—100 East 59th street, near Third avenue. Open from 9 to 6.

NORTH WESTERN DISPENSARY—No. 511 Eighth avenue.

[*St. Luke's Hospital—Fifth avenue and 54th street.*]

NORTHERN DISPENSARY—Waverley place, corner of Christopher street.

YORKVILLE DISPENSARY—Third avenue, between 83d and 84th streets.

EYE AND EAR INFIRMARY—Corner 13th street and Second avenue.

MISCELLANEOUS.

ARMORIES OF NEW YORK CITY MILITIA.—Seventh Regiment New York National Guard Armory. Over Tompkins Market, corner Seventh street and Third avenue. Fitted up and fur-

[*Seventh Regiment Armory and Tompkins Market—Third avenue.*]

nished at the expense of the companies of the regiment. The site of the armory was granted them by the consent and at the pleasure of the Common Council. Built 1859, entirely of iron. Cost $250,000.

Eighth Regiment Armory—Over Centre Market, corner Grand and Centre streets.

Twenty-Second Regiment Armory—Fourteenth street near Sixth avenue. Built 1863. Cost $150,000.

Thirty-Seventh Regiment Armory—Junction Broadway and Sixth avenue. Built 1861. Cost $200,000.

Area of the Island of Manhattan, or City of New York—22 square miles and 20,424 square yards.

A New York snowstorm gives temporary employment to eight thousand men and boys.

Assay Office—Adjoining Custom House, Pine street. Visitors admitted Wednesday from 10 to 12 A.M.

Associated Press, New York—83 Liberty street.

Arsenal—New York State—Seventh avenue, corner Thirty-fifth street.

Armory—City—Corner Elm and White streets.

Appraiser—119 Greenwich street.

Artists' Studios—Studio buildings, 51 West Tenth street, near Sixth avenue.

Association Studios—Twenty-third street and Fourth avenue.

Avenues and Streets—Avenues run North and South. Streets generally East and West. After passing Amity street the streets are named by numbers—First—Second—Third, etc., to which is prefixed "East" or "West," as the streets lie East or West of the Fifth avenue. Avenues are named by letter on the extreme East side of the town. The letters run from Avenue "A" eastward.

The avenue directly west of Avenue A is First avenue, and they continue numbering from thence westward, as Second avenue, Third avenue, and so on.

Lexington, Park, Madison and Fifth avenues are the fashionable avenues of New York. Fourth and Sixth avenues are thoroughfares and marts. Third avenue, and the easterly avenues, are more or less of this description, but not much visited by the higher classes. Eighth avenue may be classed with Fourth avenue in its character. Second avenue is a highly respectable avenue for most of its length, and a portion of it is elegant and aristocratic but not fashionable.

[*College of the City of New York—Lexington avenue.*]

The streets up town run at right angles with the avenues and are easily accessible by horse-cars, as they all cross Broadway and Fifth avenue. The irregular streets can be most easily found by referring to the map.

In the lower part of the city the streets are very irregular. A traveller in 1806 remarks in a letter to a friend—" I am perplexed to find my way through the crooked streets. The houses appear to be huddled together like trees in a forest. When I think I am travelling in the road I wish to go, I frequently find myself in one which runs in a contrary direction."

Baths.

Electric, Sun, Turkish, and other baths, 61 Lexington avenue. Russian Vapor Baths, 25 E. 14th street.

Public Free Baths.

Foot of Charles street, North River.
Foot of Fifth street, East River.

Open, under very carefully printed rules and regulations, for males on Tuesdays, Thursdays, and Saturdays, from 5 A.M. to 9 P.M., and on Sundays from 5 A.M. to 12 M. For females on Mondays, Wednesdays, and Fridays, from 5 A.M. till 9 P.M.

Banks.

Bank of Commerce,
        Nassau, corner Cedar street.
American Exchange Bank,
        128 Broadway.

For other banks, of which there are a large number, see City Register, in New York Directory.

Board of Underwriters (Marine), 49 Broadway.
Bar Association, 20 West 27th street.
Committee of the Labor Exchange Office, Castle Garden.

Confectioneries.

The best are scattered along Broadway, above Canal street. Prices generally uniform in fashionable streets.

MISCELLANEOUS. 117

COMMERCIAL REGISTER.

One is to be found in the latter part of the New York City DIRECTORY, containing the names of the principal merchants and manufacturers, and forming a complete Business Directory.

CROTON WATER WORKS.

The Croton River is forty miles distant from the City, and its current turned into an aqueduct, and conveyed to the metropolis.

[*New Croton Reservoir—In the Central Park.*]

The Croton Aqueduct Department is in the Rotunda of the City Hall—down-town Park.

THE CHIEF OFFICERS are.—

Thomas Stephens	President.
Robert L. Darragh	Assistant Commissioner.
George S. Greene	Chief Engineer.
Henry L. Robertson	Chief Clerk.
Benjamin S. Church	Assistant Engineer.

THE CROTON DAM.—The Dam is 250 feet long, and 38 feet wide, allowing a discharge of water sufficient to supply the lake, which covers an area of 400 acres. The dam is built across Croton River, about six miles from its mouth.

The Croton Aqueduct—Is thirty-two miles in length, built underground of stone and brick.

The water is carried in iron pipes over the High Bridge, which spans the Harlem River and Valley, distant eight miles from City Hall.

The Receiving Reservoir, five miles from the City Hall, by

[*Croton Water Aqueduct—"High Bridge."*]

Harlem R. R., is capable of containing 150,000,000 gallons of water.

The Distributing Reservoir, on 40th and 42d streets, is a splendid specimen of masonwork. Its architecture is in the Egyptian style.

The New Reservoir in Central Park is intended to supply a higher pressure of water for those parts of the city where the high ground renders such an improvement necessary.

The cost of the whole enterprise was over thirteen millions of dollars. When the season is remarkably dry the entire flow of the Croton River is brought into the city, and if it ever becomes necessary, resort will be had to the storage lakes in Putnam County for a supply of water for New York.

HIGH BRIDGE.—Over the Harlem River, eight miles from the City Hall. Reached by carriage or stage to Carmansville.

Docks.

Naval Dry Dock, Wallabout Bay, Brooklyn.
Take Bridge street Ferry, foot of New Chambers street.
Balance Dry Dock, between Piers 41 and 42, East river.
Sectional Dry Docks, for the purpose of lifting vessels, foot of Pike street, East river; also between Piers 42 and 43, and Piers 48 and 49, East river.

Department of Docks—Office, 348 Broadway.

Dry Dock.—To visit it take East Broadway and Dry Dock cars. See Index for "Cars."

EXPRESS.—See "Companies."—Packages can always be sent by express from the office of your hotel.

EMIGRANT LANDING DEPOT—Castle Garden.

FREE LABOR BUREAU, AND INTELLIGENCE OFFICE, 8 Clinton place.

MONEY.—American money is represented by dollars and cents, and consists of gold, silver, and copper coin. The gold coins are: the eagle, double eagle, half-eagle, quarter-eagle, and dollar, of the value of $10, $20, $5, $2.50, and $1 respectively.

The silver coins are the dollar (100 cents), the half-dollar, the quarter-dollar, and the ten cent and five cent pieces. The copper coins are of one and two cent pieces. During the long and severe civil war the Government were forced to issue a paper currency, which is still the circulating medium of the country, though fast approximating in value to gold. This Government issue is familiarly known by the name of "Greenbacks," and consists of notes in value from ten cents upwards; there is also a nickel piece of five cents. Greenbacks are made "lawful tender" by law, except for payment of duties.

There are also "National Bank" notes, an issue of private corporations, secured by a deposit of government stocks. No issue under one dollar.

MARKETS.

The two characteristic markets of the metropolis are

FULTON MARKET—Fulton street, near Fulton ferry, East river.

WASHINGTON MARKET, corner of Fulton and West streets, North river.

Visit one of these markets early in the morning.

NATURALIZATION OFFICE—First floor, 12½ City Hall.

NOVELTY WORKS—Foot of 12th street, East river.

NAVY YARD—Wallabout Bay, Brooklyn. Take Bridge street Ferry, at the foot of New Chambers street. Second avenue cars are the most eligible, but do not carry you quite to the ferry.

POST-OFFICE—Corner Nassau and Liberty streets. Open the entire day on week days.

Sundays, from 9 to 10 A.M., and from 12½ to 1½ P. M.

POSTAGE—For any part of the United States postage must be prepaid, on all letters in three cent stamps for letters of single weight; six cent stamps for double letters, and so on; news-

[*The Navy Yard—East River, Brooklyn.*]

papers, from one cent up, according to weight; small packages, like a handkerchief, or a pair of gloves, or a book, can be sent by mail, the number of stamps depending upon the number of ounces the package may weigh. Single letters throughout the city require a two cent stamp. Circulars, one cent. Stamps may be purchased at the Post-Office, or its branches, and ordinarily at book-stores and at the office of your hotel.

The Distributing Stations, connected with the Carrier's Department, are:—Station A, 100 Spring st.—B, 382 Grand st.—C, 627 Hudson st.—D, 12 Astor Place—E, 465 Eighth avenue—F, 342 Third avenue—G, 735 Seventh avenue—H, 978 Third avenue, Yorkville—K, 86th street, near Third avenue—L, 1922 Third avenue, Harlem—M, 158th street, Washington Heights.

There are letter-boxes attached to the lamp-posts every two or three blocks in the thoroughfares. All letters can be dropped in any of these. They are collected nine times a day, and promptly and safely delivered.

Articles purchased at the booksellers' or music-stores can be sent directly from there by mail or by express.

PUBLIC PORTERS—Each public porter wears a brass badge in a conspicuous place upon the person, with "public porter," and the number of his license engraved thereon.

For carrying any article in the hands half a mile or less, twenty-five cents.

If carried on a hand-cart, fifty cents.

In the same proportion for greater distances.

To charge more is a violation of the law, and subjects the offender to a penalty.

In event of overcharge, apply to the Mayor, No. 6, City Hall.

POLICE STATIONS.

156 West 20th street.
165 East 22d street.
First avenue, corner Fifth street.
221 Mercer street.
53 Spring street.
247 Madison street.
160 Chambers street.
126th street, near Third avenue.
152d street and Tenth avenue.
126 Wooster street.
City Hall, in the Park, Broadway and Chambers street.
55 Greenwich street.
300 Mulberry street.
Whitehall street, corner of State street.
120 East 35th street.

POLICE COMMISSIONERS—Office 300 Mulberry street.

The above are a few of the most accessible stations.

PRINTING-HOUSE SQUARE—Opposite City Hall Park.

An open paved space scarcely large enough to be called a square. In its vicinity are nearly all the leading newspaper establishments of the city. The *Times*, *Tribune*, and *Sun* are within the square. The *Herald*, the *World*, the *News*, the *Express*, the *Mail*, the *Staats Zeitung*, and a large number and variety of weekly and other prints in the immediate neighborhood.

A statue of Franklin ornaments the square.

PRINTING-OFFICES—The printing establishments of New York are a marvel. The sight-seer should not fail to visit some of the more important, and witness the working of the machinery and the numerous appointments connected with the issue of the large dailies of the metropolis. He should then pay a visit to "The Harpers," Franklin square—perhaps the largest establishment in the world—and to "Frank Leslie's," corner of Pearl and Elm streets, another mammoth establishment, and witness the printing of the pictorials—a very curious operation.

PRODUCE EXCHANGE—A handsome brick edifice in Whitehall street, between Water and Pearl,—a general daily meeting ground for dealers in grain, flour, produce, etc.

RAILROAD COMPANIES—For these see City Register in New York Directory.

RAILROAD GUIDE—Appleton's. Tourists had better purchase one. Price 25 cents.

SEAMEN'S EXCHANGE—187 and 189 Cherry street. A handsome four-story building, with a white stone front and a Mansard roof. It is intended to be a creditable and safe resort for Jack ashore.

STEWART'S STORE—This is a feature of the city, from its size and being a mart in itself. It occupies the entire block from Broadway to Fourth avenue, and from Ninth to Tenth streets. It is the largest retail store in the world. It is visited as a curiosity and is also a safe and convenient place for shopping. It

[*The Produce Exchange—Whitehall Street.*]

contains almost everything that is to be bought in the different varieties of stores in Broadway. Here is but one price, and there are cheap articles for those limited in purse.

SAFE DEPOSIT COMPANIES—These are admirable institutions. Valuables of larger or smaller bulk are kept here secure for a small percentage. For principal office see Index for "Companies."

SUBURBAN RAILROADS—Hudson River Railroad Depôt, for places between New York and Yonkers, Corner of Thirtieth street and Tenth avenue.

New Haven Railroad Depôt, corner Twenty-seventh street and Fourth avenue.

Hudson River and Harlem Railroad Depôt, Forty-second street and Fourth avenue. (*See illustration, page* 74.)

STEAMBOATS—The North and East River Steamboats are in their luxurious appointments, and their elegance of finish and ornamentation really palatial. To be seen at the wharves.

TIFFANY'S—This store, an exquisite establishment, is also visited as a curiosity. So full of rare and beautiful combinations of jewelry, bronzes, and ornamental articles, large and small—its interior seems an enchanted palace, while its exterior exhibits one of the finest specimens of architectural taste in the metropolis.

TELEGRAPH OFFICES—These offices are in all the principal Hotels and Railroad Depôts.

VIEW OF NEW YORK—The most comprehensive is to be seen from Brooklyn Heights—take Wall Street Ferry—and from the steeple of Trinity Church.

WHAT CAN BE BOUGHT IN BROADWAY—Everything. Some useful articles are cheaper in the avenues. See Index for "Shopping."

WHARVES.—Among the most picturesque scenes presented to the sightseer are the wharves of any city. Perhaps the most so in the world are those of New York, partly owing to their extent, the city being an island, partly to the cosmopolitan character of those employed at, or who build about them.

There are belt railways leading from and connecting some of the principal car lines, so that the wharves are easily accessible. The North river wharves, particularly those towards the lower end of the city, are the most interesting, as here there is an accumulation of home trade which gives infinite animation to the scene.

Besides the forests of shipping clustered in our harbor, the magnificent river steamboats are something to be seen only in American docks.

OMNIBUSES.

Their starting-point, terminus, and route.

Omnibuses have their route printed in large letters on the outside.

They run till 12 o'clock at night. They do not run on Sundays.

Fare, ten cents.

BROADWAY AND FIFTH AVENUE.—From Fulton Ferry to Fulton street, to Broadway, to Eleventh street, to University place, to Thirteenth street, to Fifth avenue, to Forty-seventh street. Returns same route.

BROADWAY AND FOURTH AVENUE.—From South Ferry to Broadway, to Union square, to Fourth avenue, to Thirty-second street. Returns same route.

BROADWAY, TWENTY-THIRD STREET AND NINTH AVENUE.—From South Ferry to Broadway, to Twenty-third street, to Ninth avenue, to Thirtieth street. Returns same route.

MADISON AVENUE.—From Wall street Ferry through Wall street, to Broadway, to Twenty-third street, to Madison avenue, to Fortieth street. Returns same route.

For other Omnibus routes see outside of the different vehicles.

PARKS AND SQUARES.

[*The Park at "The Battery."*]

There are numerous public squares, or so-called "parks" scattered through the metropolis; but as it is impossible to visit other places of particular interest without passing them, we give the localities of only the principal ones, and these without description. We believe that what can be left undescribed is always more fully enjoyed: description uniformly raising the expectations beyond probable realization. It is for this reason we have pursued this principle throughout the hand-book.

BATTERY.—At the lowest or southerly extremity of the city, on the Bay.

Size twelve acres. Fine trees and seats. Music in summer.

BOWLING GREEN—Just above the Battery and at the foot of Broadway. At the time of the Revolution it contained a leaden statue of George III. which the patriots demolished and converted into musket balls.

GRAMERCY PARK—Between Irving place and Lexington avenue and 20th and 21st streets.

HUDSON SQUARE—Hudson, Laight, Varick and Beach streets. This was once the "Court end" of town. The houses still remain as they were. On this square are St. John's Episcopal church, and the Laight Street church, formerly under the pastorate of Dr. Cox, the distinguished Presbyterian.

[*Washington Monument—Union Square.*]

Hudson square is now the Hudson River freight depot.

MADISON SQUARE—Seven acres—Madison avenue and Fifth avenue, east and west; 26th street and 23d street, north and south. This square is in, perhaps, the most beautiful part of the city

On the east side is Dr. Adams' Presbyterian Church. This clergyman is one of the most profound, as well as popular preachers of his denomination.

On the west side of the square is the Fifth Avenue and other fine hotels, and the Worth monument, and on the south side Broadway intersecting Fifth avenue. (*See illustration, page* 39.)

STUYVESANT SQUARE—Four acres—Both sides of Second avenue, east and west, between 17th and 15th streets, north and south.

TOMPKINS SQUARE—10¼ acres—Avenues B and A, east and west, between 10th and 7th streets, north and south.

Music in summer.

This square is especially accessible for the working classes.

THE PARK—11 acres—Broadway, Chambers street, Centre street and Park row.

In it are the City Hall and the various corporation buildings, the New Court House, and the new United States Post-Office.

[*Lincoln Monument—Union Square.*]

UNION SQUARE—3½ acres—Between Fourth avenue and Broadway, east and west, and 17th and 14th streets, north and south.

WASHINGTON SQUARE—9½ acres—University place, Waverley place, Macdougal street, and Fourth street.

This square was formerly called "Washington Parade Ground." Previously to that it was used as the "Potters'

Field," so called—that is, the pauper's burying ground, and for many years an immense number of interments took place in trenches, where now flourish its finest trees.

After it became a pleasure ground, fine residences sprung up around it, and it was a centre of fashion. The houses still remain, and in some instances are occupied by their original owners.

On the east side of the Square is the "University;" also a Dutch Reformed Church; minister, Rev. Dr. Hutton, an old and able Dutch Reformed preacher. Music in summer.

All the parks are constantly undergoing improvements, which add from year to year to their beauty and luxury.

[*Mount Sinai Hospital—Lexington Avenue.*]

PUBLIC BUILDINGS.

[*The New Post Office, in the City Hall Park.*]

Among the most conspicuous for architectural effect are:

CITY HALL, in the Park. Built in 1803–10. It is a noble edifice of admirable proportions. Its clock-tower is the finest in the country, and its clock, as a time-keeper, unsurpassed. The clock is illuminated at night.

Paintings in the Governor's room, by Trumbull, Weir, Catlin, Inman, Elliott, and others—all American artists.

Accessible during all the day.

It is an interesting fact, showing the amazing growth of the city, that the rear of this edifice is built of brown-stone, while the front and sides are of marble. No one then supposed the city would ever reach above the City Hall, and brown-stone was used for the rear as a matter of economy.

Court House—New. In the Park. Built at a fabulously exaggerated expense, and even now not finished. Its cost, including the furniture, according to the commissioner's accounts, is thus far nearly fifteen millions of dollars! It will be a monument of the extravagance, corruption and rascality of the municipal party in power at the time of its construction.

Custom House—Formerly Merchants' Exchange. Southeast corner Wall and William streets.

Constructed of blue granite; 200 feet in length, 171 in width. Fine portico of 18 Ionic columns. The interior is equally imposing. Built in 1835. Cost $1,800,000.

Castle Garden—In the Battery. Built in Colonial times for a fort. It afterwards became a fashionable resort; then a concert hall, and is now the Emigrant Depot.

New Post Office—In the Park.

Here the United States Courts will be held.

Perhaps the finest structure of the kind in America. Will cost about five millions of dollars. It consists of three stories, surmounted by a Mansard roof of the style (French Renaissance) of the Tuileries and the Hôtel de Ville. It will be ornamented by twenty fine statues, and will display large clocks at several points. The public corridor is 600 feet in length and 25 feet wide.

Present Post Office—In Nassau street, from Cedar street to Liberty street. (*See illustration, page* 87.)

This building was formerly the Middle Dutch church, of revolutionary memory. In its steeple Franklin studied and developed his electrical theories.

[*City Prisons—The " Tombs"—Centre Street.*]

THE "TOMBS," or CITY PRISON—It occupies a square between Centre, Elm, Franklin, and Leonard streets.

The prison contains 150 cells. The police and other courts are held in the building. Executions take place in the interior court. It is a massive structure, built of granite, and in the Egyptian style, and especially gloomy in appearance. Visitors are admitted on application to the keeper.

There are eleven cells especially constructed for criminals sentenced to death or imprisonment for life. This corridor is called "Murderers' Row." Each prisoner costs the county about thirty cents a day.

There are many more cells on the male than on the female side of the prison.

It was built in 1838. There is both Catholic and Protestant worship held in the Tombs.

UNITED STATES TREASURY—Corner Wall and Nassau streets.

Imposing building. White marble. Grecian architecture. One of the most substantially built edifices in the world. It is 200 feet long; 80 feet high, and 80 feet wide. At the main entrance is a flight of 18 marble steps. It has two porticos of eight Grecian columns, each 32 feet high. On this site (the old Federal Hall), Washington delivered his Inaugural Address. (*See illustration, page* 45.)

Other public buildings, all of which are costly and imposing, are indicated in the "Narrative," in "Asylums," in "Benevolent Institutions," in "Literary and Scientific Institutions," and under other headings.

[*Deaf and Dumb Institution—162d Street.*]

SUMMER RESORTS—WATERING PLACES.

The most distinguished are :—

SARATOGA SPRINGS AND LAKE GEORGE.—Via Hudson River Railroad. Distance from New York, 183 miles.

NEWPORT, Rhode Island.—Via Fall River steamboat. Pier 28, foot of Murray street.—Distance from New York, 144 miles.

LONG BRANCH, New Jersey.—Pier 32, North River, foot of Duane and Jay streets. Distance from New York, 32 miles.

WHITE MOUNTAINS.—Via New Haven Railroad. Distance from New York, 330 miles.

NIAGARA FALLS.—Via Harlem or Hudson River Railroad. Distance from New York, 450 miles.

WEST POINT.—By boat, Pier 39, North River, or by Hudson River Railroad. Distance from New York, 52 miles.

PLACES OF RESORT SHORT DISTANCES FROM TOWN OF LESSER NOTE BUT FIRST-CLASS, AND PLEASANT FOR A TRIP OF A DAY.

NEW BRIGHTON, Staten Island.—Ferry, foot of Whitehall street. Boats leave several times daily.

CONEY ISLAND.—Though not a fashionable resort, has a splendid beach, and very fine surf-bathing, and is about 10 miles from New York. By boat, Pier 1, North River, Battery place; by car, Brooklyn horse cars. Depot, 36th street, near Fifth avenue, Brooklyn.

CATSKILL MOUNTAINS.—By boat, Pier 35, North River, foot of Franklin street, or by Hudson River Railroad.

NEW ROCHELLE.—Eighteen miles, by New Haven Railroad.

HOBOKEN.—Interesting from being the place where BURR and HAMILTON fought their fatal duel. Ferry, foot of Barclay street. Boats run every fifteen minutes.

The vicinity of New York abounds in pleasant summer retreats. The summer generally comes with sudden fierceness, and precipitating the heated term, and leading every one to think of the numerous cool resorts by the seaside and on the mountain top. Then hotel proprietors of these places set actively to work, preparing for the reception of the dusty and overworked of the metropolis, who seek brief refuge from the cares of business. In the countless cosy little nooks that cluster on the Sound and Bay and inlets on the Atlantic coast, that are scattered broadcast over the valleys of New Jersey and Pennsylvania, that greet the wayfarer at every station on the railroads of the Empire State, that hide under the shadow of the mountains of New England, and that dot the vast region of the West, the hum of preparation is heard. The annual flight from the haunts of business and the hurly-burly of the metropolis is a cheerful phase in American life. The prodigious energy and untiring attention to business displayed by our people, which seem incredible to our transatlantic friends, find a necessary safety valve in the summer time, when the merchant, the broker, the manager, the speculator, the editor, *et id omne genus*, meet together in some cool, pleasant spot, to lose the cares and trials of a busy life in the lethe of a watering place, a mountain eyrie, or a quiet rural cottage.

HINTS AND NOTES.

We have endeavored to prepare and group systematically the information we have furnished for the visitor to the metropolis. But there are innumerable points on almost innumerable subjects which defy classification, but which it is an absolute necessity for the traveller to be informed about. We conceive it to be one of the important points for a Handbook or Guide to answer certain questions which naturally rise to the lips of the visitor about a thousand matters of everyday occurrence. We have devoted, therefore, considerable room to these everyday topics. They will serve the stranger better than if we had used the same space in describing the very buildings he is going to see, or in telling him what he cannot help finding out when he arrives at the spot. We have arranged even these desultory but interesting pieces of information as far as possible in alphabetical order, thus carrying out the plan with which we commenced, to present everything in that shape, so that while we give a very extensive and minute index, the possessor of the Handbook may open at any page and pass from one subject to another in the order of the alphabet. This is making everything as simple as A, B, C.

A LADY MAY WEAR, at the present time, to any entertainment, a high-necked, long-sleeved dark or black silk dress, if it be fresh and fashionably made. This is convenient to know, for there are many ladies who, in travelling, do not wish to be cumbered with the enormous trunks which are necessary to carry a set of regular party dresses. Gentlemen, at parties, must appear in full dress—*i. e.*, black dress coat and pantaloons, plain vest, and gloves.

A GLASS OF BRANDY, in an emergency, can be obtained at any apothecary. No wines, ales, or liquors are permitted to be sold in New York at any bar on Sunday. The guests of a hotel can be served with them, however, at table or in their rooms.

BARNUM'S MUSEUM, as it was, was one of the institutions of the metropolis, but exists no longer. It formerly stood on the

[*Interior of Wood's Museum—Formerly Barnum's Museum.*]

site of the Herald building. It was removed farther up town and destroyed by fire a few years ago, with most of its stock of curiosities. The killing of a tiger which had escaped into the street, by one of the policemen, was one of the incidents of the fire. The curiosities which were saved were distributed among private exhibitions, except those now included in Wood's Museum. The receipts of Barnum's Museum were at one time between four and five hundred thousand dollars a year. There was a *furore* about it all over the country, and even in Europe. People coming in town would visit it the first thing after securing their rooms at their hotel, and distinguished foreigners asked to see " Barnum."

BILLIARDS—There are billiard rooms connected with most of the hotels and large saloons and restaurants throughout the city.

BOULEVARDS—The Grand Boulevard is a continuation of Broadway, above 59th street and Eighth avenue; running diagonally to 72d street and Tenth avenue; thence continuing north to the upper end of the Island, at Harlem River. The Grand Boulevard, when completed, with its long vistas of shade-trees, will far surpass the Champs Elysées of Paris, the Unter der Linden of Berlin, or Hyde Park Lane in London.

BAY OF NEW YORK.—It is considered by some the finest in the world.

BANKS OPEN—From 10 to 3 o'clock. There is no special rule for the business offices as to hours.

BASE BALL GAMES—Every week in summer, in the various suburbs. Generally advertised in the daily papers. Go and see them.

BOAT RACES AND HORSE RACES—Are always advertised in the daily papers before they take place.

THE CITY BUDGET.—We give the following to show the curious financial operations of the Metropolis:—

The Chamberlain makes the following weekly exhibit of the city finances, showing the receipts, payments and balances of each account:—

	Balance	
	April 20.	April 30.
City Treasury	$2,964,155.89	$2,573,088.15
Sinking Fund Redemption	22,732.75	52,467.10
Sinking Fund Interest	299,345.61	125,467.26
Interest on City Stocks	34,659.68	2,402,180.60
Board of Apportionment	40,966.00	63,500.79
County Treasury	1,131,164.56	663,906.91
Total	$4,473,024.49	$5,970,700.81
	Payments.	Receipts.
City Treasury	$1,797,052.50	$1,405,984.76
Sinking Fund Redemption	3,025.84	32,760.24
Sinking Fund Interest	182,991.89	9,113.49
Interest on City Stocks	1,034.74	2,458,555.66
Board of Apportionment		22,624.79
County Treasury	700,997.91	233,740.26
Totals	$2,685,102.88	$4,162,779.20

COMMERCE, INDUSTRY, AND IMMIGRATION.

The principal branches of New York industry may be divided into three classes. The first class embraces those branches which furnish what is most indispensable to living: food, clothing, construction of buildings, and furniture.

The second class comprises: manufactures in articles of luxury, goldsmiths' work, plate, jewelry, carriages, trade in industrial articles, and implements manufactured in New York State, and the New England States.

Those most intimately connected with intellectual wants, such as printing, engraving, the paper-trade, etc., particularly remarkable in this Metropolis.

The commercial, or industrial associations, which are established in the city of New York are, besides many great railways and financial companies, the following: life insurance companies, omnibus companies, gas-lighting companies, dry dock companies, the trans-Atlantic telegraph company, fire insurance companies, express companies, various dock companies, and steamship companies. In fine, New York is the centre of an immense category of prosperous enterprises.

Custom-House Dues.

Persons arriving from foreign countries in New York have to submit to the visit of the custom-house officer before disembarking. This is apt to be disagreeable in proportion to the resistance you are disposed to show.

Since the war, duties on imported articles have been very largely increased and the examinations of travellers' baggage, formerly so slight, is now very strict.

It appears from the report of the Bureau of Statistics, lately issued, that there was in the last year, ending December 31, a large increase, both of our commerce and immigration, over the previous year. The total number of emigrants that arrived in 1871 was 346,939, of whom 204,728 were males, and 142,210 females. This is at the rate of nearly a thousand a day.

Our imports of merchandise for 1871 amounted to $572,501,-304, and of domestic exports to $415,563,658. Our export of specie, however, was $65,682,.42, or, deducting $17,399,415 of specie and bullion imported, the balance of the precious metals exported amounted to $48,282,927. The total commerce in imports and exports, including re-exports of foreign merchandise and specie, amounted to the vast sum of $1,127,943,676. The total imports for the year 1871 exceeded those of 1870 $103,078,902, and the exports amounted to $57,300,178 over those of 1870. Our commerce increased in one year, imports and exports included, $160,379,080.

City Wall.—The only city wall was one long since demolished, built across Wall street to keep out the Indians.

Calls and Callers.—Calls of ceremony are made between two and half-past four o'clock. Morning calls between eleven and twelve, evening calls between eight and nine; evening calls may be prolonged to ten or half-past ten. Morning calls are made in simple walking costume, afternoon and evening calls in more dressy suits, with either long or short skirts.

COURTS ARE OPEN TO THE PUBLIC at all times. No *fees* necessary; secure a seat if you can.

CITY LIMITS extend over the entire island of Manhattan, and the Central Park Commissioners have also control over the southerly portion of Westchester county.

COLLEGES OF THE CITY:—
Columbia College.
Free Academy, or College of the City of New York.
University.
Medical Colleges.
Female Medical College.
Theological Seminaries.

COLLECTIONS OF OBJECTS OF ART.—These are to be seen at Art Galleries (see index), and at Goupil's, Tiffany's, and at other public places which have no permanent locality, but are advertised freely in the daily newspapers.

CARTS AND CARMEN.—The prices for loading, transportation, and unloading of goods, wares and other articles, are fixed by law.

When the distance exceeds half a mile, and is within a mile, one-third more shall be added to the regular rates, and in the same proportion for any greater distance. Asking and receiving more than the legal rates is a violation of the law, and punishable accordingly. In any difficulty apply to the Mayor. Each cart is numbered. Take a memorandum of the number before you lose sight of your goods.

On the first of May, or "moving-day," the demand for cartage is so great, that exaggerated prices have to be paid to get your goods and chattels moved at all. This is the only exception to the general rule.

CHOICE OF LOCALITY.—Any of the streets crossing Broadway, either side, are eligible as a residence as far down town as Waverley Place (though few would care to go below 20th street), and as far up town as you choose to go. Also all the avenues, west of First avenue, except Third, Sixth, and Eighth. These are occupied by shop-keepers, artisans, etc. The fashionable streets for those who are able to live in them are easily distinguished by their beauty and elegance.

CRYSTAL PALACE.—The Crystal Palace once stood on the Sixth avenue side of the 42d street reservoir. That spot is now a small and pretty public square—called Reservoir Park.

CHURCHES.—(For list of the most prominent, see page 78.)

N. B.—The variety in style of our churches proclaims the supremacy of the public conscience, which imposes no belief on any man, but lets the congregations of any creed build as they like, if they can pay for it.

DISTANCES IN THE CITY—Twenty blocks make a mile. This means the *length* of the blocks, including the streets, and not a square block.

DISTANCES ACROSS THE FERRIES.

South, 1,066 yards.
Fulton, 731 yards.
Catharine, 745 yards.
Williamsburg, 952 yards.
Staten Island, 6,418 yards.

The length of the blocks between First and 121st streets, varies from 181 to 212 feet; distance between the avenues, from 405 to 920 feet.

WIDTH OF STREETS AND AVENUES.

The avenues are all 100 feet wide, excepting Lexington and Madison, which are 75, and Fourth avenue, above 34th street, which is 140 feet wide.

The numerical streets are all 60 feet wide, excepting 14th, 23d, 34th, 42d, and eleven others, north of these, which are 100 feet wide.

DRINKING SALOONS—From the most aristocratic to the most disreputable, are scattered through all parts of the Metropolis, and are a feature of New York life quite incomprehensible to the European.

DIRECTORY.—There is but one New York Directory. It is published every year in July with revisions, and comprehends all names with business address and private residence, and an immense amount of local statistics and information.

[*Academy of the Sacred Heart—Tenth Avenue.*]

Dinner Hour.—The dinner hour in New York is from five to half-past six. Evening calls may be made by gentlemen and ladies as early as eight o'clock.

Detectives.—The Detective force in New York is an invaluable institution. Its members are shrewd and courageous, and it is an art with them to appear like private citizens.

Dorlan's Oysters—Are to be had at a stand in Fulton Market. His "Saddle Rocks," cooked in various ways, are very celebrated. If near the market, try them.

Elevators—These are now introduced not only in all the principal hotels, but also in the large buildings down town which are let for offices.

Fashionable Dressmakers—Their charges are so exorbitant that many ladies in the upper circles prefer to buy patterns, and, with the aid of a plain seamstress and a sewing-machine, make their own dresses. See daily papers for seamstresses' advertisements.

Patterns, of all kinds, can be bought at stores where nothing else is kept. See daily papers for advertisements of these.

Fashion Plates—There are many monthly magazines, and some weekly papers, devoted to these special illustrations, but altogether the best descriptions accompany those in *Frank Leslie's Lady's Magazine*. These descriptions are minute and intelligible. Single numbers can be bought at any book-store or book-stand. *Frank Leslie's Lady's Journal*, a weekly paper, also contains excellent illustrations, as also *Harper's Bazar*.

Fashion.—The approach of summer dispels all thoughts of gas-light receptions. These are succeeded by a grand display of street-fashions, every Sunday, on Fifth avenue, and later, by a still more brilliant display, at the races at Jerome Park. All New York, young and old, on the tip-toe of expectation, impatiently wait for the opening of the Jerome Park races.

French Cooking—Is now fully appreciated and practised in

New York. The first-class hotels all employ French cooks; so do the clubs, as well as rich private families.

FASHIONABLE NEWSPAPERS—There are several of these weeklies. They are mainly interesting from furnishing the most minute and elaborate descriptions of some of the costly parties, receptions, and weddings, given in the metropolis, and for their gossip and small talk about so-called fashionable people. They cannot be relied on as to the social status of individuals and families, being got up entirely in the Jenkins style of literature. The stranger will, however, be entertained in looking at some of these issues.

FOREIGN MONEY—Is not current, but can be exchanged at exchange offices. You will find many of these in Wall street, and along Broadway.

FRENCH AND GERMAN WAITERS.—There is a large mixture of these, with Irish and English waiters, in most of the hotels and restaurants.

FRUIT STORES—The finest are principally in Broadway, and among the business streets down town. Home and foreign fruits, fresh and dried, and in the greatest perfection, are to be had at these stores at all seasons. Also every species of nuts, both American and foreign.

FURNISHED APARTMENTS.—This has become a very customary way for letting rooms. Those to be let, without board, are advertised in the daily payers.

FURNISHED HOUSES.—There are splendid, as well as merely comfortable, furnished houses to be let by the year—all at an extravagant price, however. See daily newspapers' advertising columns.

GERMAN EMIGRATION—The Hamburg papers report that emigration of Germans to the United States (1872), from Mecklenburg, is of such a remarkable character that several villages are almost depopulated. Forty-five hundred Mecklenburgers passed through Hamburg last year on their way to this country, and large numbers are preparing to follow them this season. The same can be said of other parts of Germany. It is shown by the statistics that the German element in the United States, fed by continual accessions from the Fatherland, is increasing relatively faster than any other.

Grocery Stores—These stores, which occupy the first floor of many corner buildings, supply most families of all classes with every species of food with the exception of butchers' meat. The sale of the latter, with most of the vegetables, poultry, game, and fish, is monopolized by the markets and "shop butchers."

Great Thoroughfares—Broadway is the principal thoroughfare of New York, and extends from the extreme lower end of the metropolis to its limit at the end of the island, whence it is continued through the suburban city of Yonkers, a distance of about twenty miles. This street is policed and lighted its whole length. In the unbuilt or country districts it is guarded by mounted policemen. If there be a unique street architecturally, it is Broadway. The entire disregard of unity, the competition in costly and massive buildings, the diversity of material, as well as adornment, combine to make it as a highway of commerce, the paragon of the world, and in every pillar, façade and cornice proclaim it the special result of the energy and enterprise of a free, thriving people.

The Bowery—Begins at Chatham street, and extends until it meets Third and Fourth avenues at Sixth street. It is filled with stores of all kinds, where cheaper goods are sold than in Broadway. Most of the stores are kept by Jews and Germans. The shops of the former are open on Sunday in this thoroughfare. Almost all the German places of amusement are in the Bowery.

Canal Street—Which runs east and west, from the North

River to East Broadway, crossing the Bowery, Broadway, and Hudson street, is one of the widest streets and busiest thoroughfares in the metropolis; but being now " down town " it partakes more or less of the character of the down-town commerce and trade.

For other thoroughfares see " Avenues and Streets."

EIGHTH AVENUE—This avenue joins Hudson street at Abingdon square, and constitutes one large and busy thoroughfare southward. On the north it runs up a broad and strait drive to Macomb's Dam, Harlem river, or one hundred and fifty-fifth street. Hudson street is an old street and exhibits less of the foreign element in its inhabitants than any other thoroughfare in New York. An old, respectable and substantial class of trades-people occupy it, and the streets in its neighborhood, which are well built up, with here and there even handsome houses. Here is evidently considerable wealth, though far removed from any fashionable vicinity or associations.

SIXTH AVENUE—Is much frequented by ladies of the highest class for shopping. Here are excellent markets and grocery stores. One of the finest street views in the city is from either corner of Sixth avenue and Twenty-third street, looking east and west through the latter street. This view increases in beauty until you reach Broadway.

GAMBLING HOUSES—These are of two classes, the high and the low. It is dangerous for any one to enter either. Persons are enticed into the low houses to become victims. The high-class houses are on their dignity and solicit no one. But if you enter, woe be to you. There are no places so seductive as these houses, and the misery they create is *deadly*. The " day " gambling houses are down town among business marts.

GYMNASIUMS—See the popular advertisements. Excellent ones abound in the metropolis.

How to stop a stage or car when you wish to get out: In

the omnibus pull the strap which runs along the top. In the car speak to the conductor when you give him your fare, and tell him where you wish to get off.

Harlem River—This river, with Spuyten Duyvel creek, connects the East River with the Hudson, and forms the northern boundary of New York. The Harlem is a beautiful river with verdurous and wooded banks and bordered with elegant residences, and spanned by stately bridges and plied by pretty steamboats and other craft.

Hints on Accepting Invitations—If you are invited to an entertainment and you find the letters " R. S. V. P." in the corner of the card or note, be sure to answer it, accepting or declining, and in no case alter your determination afterwards. If the hour is indicated, do not go before that hour. In arriving at the house, ask the man who shows you up the steps at what hour the carriage must be ordered for you to leave.

If you are invited to dine, be punctual to the minute. If to an evening entertainment, and the hour is not designated, do not go before ten o'clock.

At all entertainments the lady of the house is the first person you will see on entering the rooms. She is always near the drawing-room door to receive her guests. After receiving an invitation it is customary to call in acknowledgment of the courtesy within a week after the entertainment has taken place.

Hell Gate and the East River Improvement.—Few people are aware of the stupendous work going on at Hell Gate and of the important results that may be expected to ensue from it. The removal of the rocks there, so as to make a perfectly free and safe channel for the largest vessels, was a vast undertaking. In this age, however, hardly anything seems impossible to engineering skill. In view, therefore, of the importance of opening a free and safe channel for the commerce of New

York by the way of Long Island Sound and the East River, the government resolved to remove the Hell Gate obstructions. The work was commenced a little more than two years ago, and it is believed that in less than two years more the whole will be completed. It is under the charge of Major-General John Newton, of the United States Engineer Corps. A vast deal of rock has already been blasted out and cleared away. Of about one hundred and sixty-five thousand cubic yards of rock to be removed, at least forty two thousand yards have been taken out. For removing the rest the rock is being tunnelled and pierced in every direction. When this is accomplished a tremendous blast will be made with seven thousand pounds of nitro-glycerine, equal in force to seventy thousand pounds of gunpowder. The

Excavations Under the East River, Hell Gate.

explosion will be a small earthquake. The details of the work are exceedingly interesting to scientific men. But the important fact is with regard to the results that must follow to the commerce of the city and to the improvement of the upper part of the island. When the largest steamship in the European trade can come safely to this port through Hell Gate and by way of Long Island Sound, thus saving time and sometimes avoiding danger by the outer passage, we may expect a portion of the business at least will be located far up town; and when, in addition to the clearing of Hell Gate, a large ship canal and a fine system of docks shall be made, by the Harlem River and Spuyten Duyvel, to connect the Sound and East River with the Hudson River, there will be, no doubt, a surprising change in the business localities of New York.

HOTEL COACHES—These are equally respectable with the hacks for taking travellers to or from their specific hotels, and much cheaper, for you have only to pay for your own seat.

HOLIDAYS IN NEW YORK.

THANKSGIVING-DAY is celebrated in every household in New York by a particularly good dinner, but not with the absolute zest of the New England feast. Great numbers of New Yorkers go into New England to spend the day with relations at their old homes.

THE FOURTH OF JULY.—The great national holiday is a day of unexampled confusion in the metropolis. The poorest boy or girl has, at least, a handful of fire-crackers, and the majority of private citizens have a display of small fireworks in their yards in the evening, while in the parks, and especially at the City Hall, the exhibition is one of surpassing splendor. The firing of pistols and crackers on every hand is heard at daybreak, simultaneously with the firing of guns from the Battery, the

Forts, the shipping in the harbor, and the Navy Yard. The excitement knows no abatement until midnight.

Washington's Birth-day is celebrated by a parade of all the military companies of the city, and a universal rejoicing; but, unlike the 4th of July, the day is characterized by the utmost decorum and dignity.

Evacuation-day.—The day the British evacuated New York is celebrated like Washington's Birth-day, but with less general feeling.

New Year's Day.—This is specially a New York institution, for it originated with the Dutch settlers, and is maintained with unabated enthusiasm, especially by the fashionable classes. Ladies stay at home to receive calls, and gentlemen have the undisputed use of the thoroughfares and streets from nine o'clock in the morning till midnight. Houses are put in the finest order in preparation for the day, and every one is in their best dress, best spirits, and best looks; and the most elaborate tables, loaded with every delicacy, are prepared. It is the great festival day of New York.

Christmas Day is also universally observed, especially among the children, to whom a Christmas party and Christmas tree are a matter of course.

On all these holidays business is entirely suspended as on Sunday.

The religious holidays of Episcopalians and Roman Catholics are celebrated here as elsewhere.

St. Patrick's Day is the great holiday of Irish emigrants. They parade the streets with military companies, music and banners.

The Orangemen now also have their parades, as do the Germans, while the various benevolent societies, target companies, and other companies, keep the city gay with their turn-outs.

How to Descend at the Right Spot from a Stage or Car.—If you wish to stop at a street on your car or omnibus route, whose locality you do not know, request the stage-driver or car conductor, when you hand him your fare, to let you know when he reaches there.

How to Get a Daily Paper.—They are to be bought in all hotels in the morning and at stands in the streets, at or near depots and ferries, and of newsboys as they pass along, and in the steam cars and ferry-boats, and can be seen in the reading-rooms of many hotels.

Information bureau, for friends of arriving emigrants—Castle Garden.

If You are in a Hurry and wish to Catch a Train—Take a cab at a hack-stand, to be seen along any of the parks or squares, on the thoroughfares. The omnibuses and cars have to stop frequently, which takes up a great deal of time; see "Hacks and Hackmen" for prices.

If You Choose to take the Trouble of Seeing to Your Own Baggage—One trunk, one bag, and one bundle for each person can be put on your carriage free of charge.

If You leave an Article in an omnibus or car, and remember the *number* of the conveyance, go to its depot. See index for omnibuses and cars. There is a good chance of your recovering it. If not, there is no other way but to advertise it with promise of a reward. See first column in morning *Herald* for these kind of advertisements.

Ice Water can be had for the asking at all railroad depots, at restaurants—in fact, everywhere.

Extension of the City of New York since 1836: At that period the Astor House, which was opened first of June in that year, was considered "up town."

Immigration—From the 1st of January to the 31st of March, 1872, 12,497 persons arrived in New York from the German

States—against 3,948 from Ireland, 7,554 from England, and 1,368 from France. The excess of German immigration was a remarkable feature in the returns of 1869-70, but the French war stopped the tide for the ensuing year. It is now setting in again with remarkable vigor, the German arrivals this year already outnumbering the Irish three to one. Another noticeable point is the unusual increase in the number of skilled laborers who are coming in; the aggregate being 3,570 for the months of January, February and March, against a total of 6,241 unskilled workmen—and if to these be added the number of 3,239 farmers who have arrived during the same period, the common laborers who follow no other avocation than that of the hewers of wood and the drawers of water are actually in a minority. This is a good sign. It shows that the careful farmer and the skilled mechanic are beginning to take the places of the ignorant peasant and the pauper, and that the general character of the immigration will add to our national strength. Another fact, interesting to students of social problems, is the rapid increase of the Protestant over the Roman Catholic element. Great Britain, exclusive of Ireland, has sent us 7,554 immigrants since January; the German States and the Scandinavian countries together have sent more than 13,000; and the Dutch and Belgians number about 400—making a total of over 20,000, out of the whole immigration of 28,000 for three months, who are chiefly of the Protestant faith. The religious enthusiasts will find food for thought and speculation in these statements.

The majority of the immigrants, of all classes, are between the ages of fifteen and forty, and there is a marked disproportion between the numbers of the males and the females—the total of the former being 19,316, and of the latter, 8,884. The principal trades represented are those of the carpenter, the mason, the tailor, the shoemaker and the baker, and there is room enough and work enough for all, provided they are wise

HINTS AND NOTES.   155

enough to leave the crowded seaports, and, like the Germans, find their new homes in the places where their labor is always in demand.

IMMIGRATION—Comparative Protestant and Catholic: 20,000 out of the whole immigration of 28,000 for the months of January, February and March for 1872 are Protestants. See previous paragraph.

LETTER STAMPS—Can be bought at any stationery or book store. A few can be obtained at the office of your hotel, or at an apothecary, generally at a corner grocery.

LETTER-BOXES—There are letter-boxes on corner lamp-posts every block or two in all the thoroughfares, and in all the first-class hotels, and in railroad depots.

[*Fire Department—Steam Fire-Engine.*]

LABORERS—Nearly all the laborers in New York, as in the other large cities of the United States, are foreigners. There is no *class* of Americans in our cities below that of the mechanic and artisan. Education and foreign immigration keeps the American in this desirable position.

MESSENGERS

Can be sent from your hotel and from various other points on any errands. The charge is ordinarily 25 cents.

METROPOLITAN FIRE DEPARTMENT.—Up to 1865 all the Fire Companies were volunteers. It is now a force under the control of the State Government, and the members receive good salaries. The drilling of the Fire Department may be compared to that of the Military Department in carefulness and exactness.

MAY ANNIVERSARIES.

With the month of May, smiling May, as from childhood we have been in the habit of hearing it named, come also the religious anniversaries. From time immemorial, and in almost all lands, May has been the favorite month for religious reunion.

The city of New York is a favorite religious centre. Our religious societies as well as our enterprising merchants reveal an affection for the great City. If here sin abounds, so also do empire and wealth. The money which is given freely for every laudable enterprise has never been grudgingly bestowed on the churches and the other kindred associations. The principal Societies represented are: the American Home Missionary Society, the American Seamen's Friend Society, the American Female Guardian Society, the National Temperance Society, the American Tract Society, the American Bible Society, the American and Foreign Christian Union, and the American Congregational Union.

HINTS AND NOTES. 157

All these associations are representatives of the religious life of our people.

[*The Morgue, or Dead House—Interior view.*]

At the anniversary season this city fills up with strangers, and clergymen and laymen come hither to discuss measures for the future progress of their work.

Morgue.—It is situated at the foot of 26th street, East River. It receives dead unrecognized bodies which have been found in the rivers or within the city limits. It is open to the public from morning to night. Bodies are detained there three days, unless claimed sooner.

Money.—Twenty cents American money is equal to ten pence English money and one franc French money.

First of May or Moving Day in the Metropolis.

It is a pandemonium in New York. The poor go from the cellar or garret of one tenement-house to another, wealthy people up town pack trunks, cases, and boxes for the country, or change for a more eligible location, or to obtain cheaper rates of rent in town. All landladies are less amiable than usual, and most are furious. Matrons lose their temper through the din and dust of the general commotion. Servants enjoy the privilege of reckless demolition. Young children cry, and larger ones help servants to break. Heads of families ache, and their lungs are smothered, and their throats are choked with dust. Countless Micawbers pocket the curses of their enraged landlords, who themselves can pocket nothing. And so the day wears on in every part of the city. The carriers and carmen reap the harvest. Eight, ten and fifteen dollars per load are the prices, and furniture wagons are scarce even at these rates. Some are engaged weeks before. At night people find themselves away from their old home—if one can be said to have a home under conditions of yearly migration—and in a strange place. Papa goes "round the corner," feeling very blue. Mamma can find nothing she needs for the children, and the dear children sit about on the floor in a most lugubrious and lachrymose condition, bewailing the fall of china angels and the breaking of little playthings. Such is life on May-day in New York.

Municipal Divisions of the City—New York is divided into Twenty-two Wards, which are subdivided into Three Hundred and Forty Election Districts.

State Assembly Districts are represented by those for Aldermen and Assistant Aldermen.

Police and Civil Justices' Districts consist of eight districts.

School Districts consist of seven districts.

The only *ward* officers now elected by the people of the city, are Trustees of Common Schools—one for each ward—at each charter election.

MEASURES, WEIGHTS, ETC.—The English measures which we use are not gauged with the scientific accuracy of the French. Thus the English yard, which is one-tenth less than the French "metre," is an arbitrary measure and not the *unit of length*, which is the ten-millionth part of the spherical distance from the pole to the equator, and which the French call the "metre."

WEIGHTS—The English pound is in use with us—is equal to the French "litre."

MEASURING CAPACITY—The measure of capacity is the quart.

THERMOMETRIC SCALE—Fahrenheit's scale is used in the United States. It differs from the "centigrade" thermometers used in France. Thus, 32° or freezing point in Fahrenheit is zero in the Centigrade, and 212° or boiling point in Fahrenheit is 100° in the Centigrade.

NEW BUILDINGS IN NEW YORK.

Building, if it goes on at the rate it has done for the past five years—that is, 2,000 houses per annum, will make a continuous line of brick and mortar from the Battery to Washington Heights.

That the visitor may fully comprehend this we give a description of the principal public buildings in course of erection in this city. The greater number are to be devoted to educational and benevolent purposes. Some of those referred to below, when finished, will present the finest specimens of architectural skill. There are at all times a number of hotels and factories building in the upper wards, and numerous extensive warehouses are to be seen in progress and upon which workmen are busily engaged. Tenement houses of the better class, and handsome private residences are also to be observed in course of construction along the avenues up to and beyond Central Park.

New York, the empress city of our country in wealth, is equally so in architectural munificence. The peculiar bent of its development shows that it exhibits none of the hackneyed curbing lines of European cities. In point of private effort it surpasses any city in the world. When the newcomer wanders uptown and sees the stately brown stone and marble mansions at every step, his longing to see one huge palace must be checked in the idea that we own no kings or princes here; that the wealth he sees is that of individual citizens of a great nation, with just a vote like their poorer neighbors.

The Lenox Library—The city of New York will soon be provided with another free library, and in the same building are to be galleries of paintings and a museum, for which the citizens will be indebted to the munificence of Mr. James Lenox, a gentleman who has devoted many years to the collection of rare and valuable books, manuscripts, paintings, statuary, and other works of art and antiquities. The building, which is on Fifth avenue, and is to cover the whole front of the block between 70th and 71st streets, is advanced to the second story. Its length is 198 feet and 114 feet in depth. The modern French style of architecture has been adopted, but the entire exterior of the edifice is to have a unique and impressive appearance. The edifice consists of two wings, divided by the court-yard; and in the far end a large hall. The only ornamentation of exterior are pediments and capitals of columns. Busts of Minerva and other allegorical figures are placed on pedestals, and so arranged as to add to the effect of the general appearance. In the two stories of the south wing will be situated the library proper and reading room. The second story is to consist of two rooms, same size as those on first, and a hall, besides a picture gallery forty by sixty feet. In the north wing is the Museum and committee room, and the third story or attic is to be used as another picture gallery. The library, according to the charter and design of Mr. Lenox, is to be open at all reasonable hours for general use, free of expense.

Strangers may be interested in the style in which our Public Schools are built, arranged, and conducted. The Department of Education includes:—

Board of Education.
School Commissioners.
Standing Committees.
School Inspectors, and
School Trustees.

NEW PUBLIC SCHOOLS—Besides the Normal College, the Board of Education have approved of plans and accepted proposals for the erection of five new school buildings in different parts of the city. Three of these houses are to be ready for occupation on the 1st of September, and the other two about the beginning of next year. The building at the corner of Sheriff and Stanton streets, in the Eleventh ward, No. 22, is among the former. The main building is 55 feet by 150 feet, and the extension 40 feet by 44 feet. There are four stories and cellar.

The public school buildings are in architectural design nearly all alike, and there is no departure from the uniform rule in this structure nor in the others to be mentioned.

The buildings are provided with over thirty wardrobes. The staircases are black walnut.

MONUMENTS—Many interesting tombstones and relics of former ages will be found in the old graveyards surrounding Trinity Church and St. Paul's, a few of which our artist has sketched in these pages.

OTHER EDUCATIONAL SCHOOLS—The two other schools to be ready for occupation on the 1st of September are one on the south side of 57th street, in the Nineteenth ward, and the other on Fifth street, in the Seventeenth ward. Both are of the same class as the one just described.

St. Michael's Roman Catholic Schools—Two large edifices are about completed—one for a grammar school for girls and the other for boys. There is besides a preparatory school, all three are connected, forming a massive pile of buildings. The building on Ninth avenue, near 31st street, is intended for girls.

The boys' grammar school is on 32d street.

[*Grave of Charlotte Temple.*]

[*Tomb of Captain Lawrence, of the "Chesapeake."*]

HINTS AND NOTES. 163

GERMAN SAVINGS BANK—The directors of the German Savings Bank in the city of New York have nearly completed a very costly and imposing building, at the corner of 14th street and Fourth avenue.

ELEVENTH WARD SAVINGS BANK—The new building for this institution, situated at the corner of Avenue C and Seventh street, has just been completed. The structure is built of iron and is three stories high, with French roof.

[*Tomb of Albert Gallatin.*]

[*Tomb of Alexander Hamilton.*]

Catholic Church on Ward's Island—The desire to accommodate as far as possible the inmates of the Emigrant refuge in the exercise of their religious duties, has induced the Commissioners of Emigration to approve the plans prepared by Messrs. Renwick & Sands, architects, for the erection of a Catholic Church on Ward's Island. The work on it has already commenced, and it is expected to be finished in about six months from this date.

[*Tomb of General Montgomery.*]

The Hebrew Industrial School—The Asylum building was not large enough to allow the requisite arrangements for workshops to be made. Accordingly the society is erecting a building on the lot in the rear of the asylum especially for this purpose.

THIRD JUDICIAL COURT HOUSE—The new court house and prison for the Third district are commenced, on the ground adjoining Jefferson Market, Sixth avenue, and are intended to take the place of the old building now in use for similar purposes.

The style of architecture is French Gothic; the material used so far is Philadelphia brick trimmed with Ohio yellow stone.

NEW JAIL—The new jail, to front on Tenth street, will have two stories and be 128 feet in length and 45 feet high. This large building is to be in part occupied by the clerks attached to the courts, and furnish accommodation also to the detachment of police assigned to duty in the precinct.

NEW YORK OPHTHALMIC HOSPITAL—The New York Ophthalmic Hospital, incorporated in April, 1852, is now ready for occupation at the corner of Third avenue and Twenty-third street.

THE NEW MASONIC HALL—Among the most noteworthy buildings in course of construction in the city, is Masonic Hall, at the corner of Sixth avenue and Twenty-third street. It fronts 141 feet on the street and runs 100 feet on the avenue. The massive construction and grand proportions of this edifice have already attracted no small share of public attention.

ST. LUKE'S HOME FOR INDIGENT FEMALES—St. Luke's Home for Indigent Females has been in existence about twenty years. It is at present on Hudson street, and its doors are open to persons of respectability in reduced circumstances, and who are members of the Episcopal Church. The new building just ready for occupation is on the north-east corner of Madison avenue and Eighty-ninth street, one block from Central Park, and two blocks only from one of the principal entrances to the Park. It is four stories high. The style is mediæval Gothic, with Mansard roof and three towers.

CHURCH OF THE BELOVED DISCIPLE—This church fronts 57 feet on Eighty-ninth street, and is 100 feet deep. It is nearly finished. The style of architecture is Gothic; the material used is Buena Vista stone, and brick for the side walls.

OLD LADIES' HOME OF THE BAPTIST CHURCH, on Sixty-eighth street, near Fourth avenue. The ground upon which the Home stands runs through the entire block and has a front of 125 feet.

ST. JOSEPH'S HOME FOR THE AGED—The trustees in charge of this institution, in charge of the Sisters of Charity, have completed their new building on the site of the old Home on Fifteenth street.

The new U. S. Post Office and the new Roman Catholic Cathedral exceed in magnificence any other buildings in the metropolis.

The NEW Court House has nothing to boast of but *size.*

NAMES OF STREETS AND AVENUES are still very generally printed on little strips, and nailed on the houses at every corner. At the same time the improved plan is adopted through the city of painting the name of the street on the glass of the corner lamp-post.

NORTH, EAST AND HARLEM RIVER AND SOUND BOATS constantly ply those waters, giving a remarkably gay and busy aspect to the scene. See Index for "Steamboat Travel."

NEW YORK CITY TAXES FOR 1872—The Board of Apportionment directed the raising, by tax, during 1872, on real and personal property, $30,437,513 01, as follows:—

Valuation of the estates, real and personal,
   subject to taxation in the city and county
   of New York in the year 1871..........$1,076,253,633 00
Tax at the rate of 2¾ per cent on such valuation.. 29,596,974 91
Excess of the quota of state tax for county
   over the amount charged on county for
   state taxes in the year 1870:—

State tax in 1872............	$5,746,049 32	
State tax in 1870............	4,904,501 22	
		840,548 10

Total to be raised by tax..............	$30,437,523 01

Of this $14,915,777 75 is apportioned for the following purposes for 1872:—

State tax, including State tax for Common Schools to be paid by the County of New York.....................................	$5,745,049 32
Interest on bonds and stocks of the County of New York...........................	2,412,670 00
Interest on bonds and stocks of the City of New York.............................	6,072,637 74
Principal of bonds and stocks as may become due and payable from taxations within the year 1872.............................	685,420 69
Total.............................	$14,915,777 75

NATURAL FLOWERS—Fresh natural flowers can be bought at the flower-stores which are scattered through Broadway. These are made into bouquets or garlands, or arranged to order. Here you can select the rarest exotics, or the wild-flowers of the woods, or the simple old-fashioned garden flowers of the country homesteads. You can buy as little as *one* flower if you wish.

Men, women, and children stand on the steps of hotels, and on the side-walks, here and there, with baskets of prettily arranged and sweet-smelling small bouquets for sale—frequently as low as ten cents.

Stores for the sale of plants of all kinds are to be found in Broadway. The plants are sometimes placed growing in very ornamental pots and baskets.

NEWSPAPERS.—The principal morning papers are the *Herald*,

[*Street Flower-Girl.*]

Tribune, Times, World, and *Sun.* Principal evening papers are the *Post, Commercial, Express, Mail,* and *News.* The principal weekly illustrated papers are *Harper's Weekly, Frank Leslie's Weekly, The Lady's Journal,* and *Harper's Bazar.*

NEW YORK BAR—There are between 3,000 and 4,000 lawyers in the metropolis. They generally all make a good living. The prominent members of the profession clear from ten to twenty-five thousand dollars a year. There is not the *esprit de corps* among lawyers here that is observable in most other cities. The lack of this feeling is not confined to lawyers. It is noticeable throughout all the "liberal professions."

HINTS AND NOTES.

ORGAN-GRINDERS AND STREET-BEGGARS—Thousands of children are annually exported from Italy to the United States for the purpose of making them organ-grinders and street-beggars, of whom a multiplicity are to be seen in New York. A bill has been brought before the Italian Parliament, designed to put a stop to this disgraceful traffic in children. It punishes with five years' imprisonment all persons exporting children under twelve years of age to foreign countries, under any pretext.

OUT-DOOR STATUES AND MONUMENTS—Equestrian statue of Washington, Union Square; statue of Lincoln, Union Square; General Worth (Monument), Madison Square.

THE NEW FRANKLIN STATUE.

The new bronze statue of BENJAMIN FRANKLIN has just been erected in Printing-House Square. It was cast from a model designed by Captain DE GROOT, who designed the huge VANDERBILT monument in St. John's Park. The statue is a gift from the designer to the Press of the city.

There are some important monuments in St. Paul's Churchyard and in Trinity Churchyard.

There is a good deal of fine statuary in Central Park which the visitor will discover on going over the grounds.

PHOTOGRAPHY.—Every species of sun-picture is taken in New York from the tin-type at 25 cents to the elaborate imperial photograph touched up to imitate fine ivory painting at a cost of fifteen to fifty dollars. The photograph galleries make quite a display along Broadway, an exhibition of many fine specimens of the art being placed conspicuously at the entrances on the street. In some of the principal galleries a few rare and costly paintings may be seen, besides a large number of admirable specimens of photographic art. The stranger must spend a morning in these galleries—free admittance.

POPULATION OF NEW YORK PROPER is about one million.

PRICES AT THE HOTELS in New York do not vary with the seasons. They range from $2 to $5 per day, which includes no extras.

Hotels on the European plan cost according to your orders.

[*Interior of the Café Brunswisk—Fifth Avenue.*]

PUBLIC AND PRIVATE DINNERS AND SUPPERS can be given at any hotel whether you live there or not. Delmonico's Restaurant, corner Fifth avenue and 14th street, is a favorite place for such entertainments. They are got up with any degree of elegance you choose to pay for, and without any trouble to yourself, except to loosen your purse-strings.

The Café Brunswick, under the Hotel of that name, is also a fashionable place for these entertainments, No. 223 Fifth avenue, corner Madison Square and 26th street.

Police—All the streets and suburbs are well guarded by policemen. There are also mounted police ranging through the upper part of the city and the lower part of Westchester county to the distance of twenty miles from the Battery.

Places and Sights which, among others, a Stranger should See.

Battery.
Blackwell's Island and Randall's Island.
Broadway from near the Worth monument.
Brooklyn Heights.
Central Park.
Fifth avenue from corner of Twenty-seventh street.
Fifth avenue from corner of Thirty-fourth street.
Grand Central Depôt.
Greenwood Cemetery.
High Bridge.
Jews' Synagogue.
Markets.
New Roman Catholic Cathedral.
Opera Houses.
Photograph Galleries.
Printing-Offices and Machinery.
Trinity Cathedral—ascend to top of steeple.
Wall street.
Wharves and Docks.
Woodlawn Cemetery.

RACES.

JEROME PARK RACES—Fordham. Take Harlem Accommodation Train, or, which is much pleasanter but more expensive, drive out in a carriage.

[*Jerome Park Race Course.*]

These races are fashionable, and attended by ladies in very dressy carriage suits.

FASHION COURSE—Near Jamaica, L. I. Ferry foot of East Thirty-fourth street to railroad depôt. You can go by rail or drive out in a carriage.

FLEETWOOD PARK TROTTING COURSE—Morrisania. You can go by Harlem Accommodation Train or drive in carriage.

PROSPECT PARK RACES—Brooklyn. Of easy access by horse-car or carriage.

All the races take place late in spring or early summer, and autumn, and are fully advertised with all particulars in the daily papers.

Religious Inteligence

And Notes relating to all sects are to be found in the Sunday morning papers. A very full report of sermons by the leading clergymen of all denominations appears every week in Monday's papers.

Religious Newspapers—Among these are:—
Catholic Freeman's Journal.
Christian Union (Henry Ward Beecher's paper).
Church Weekly—a "Free Church and State" paper.
Evangelist (Presbyterian).
Jewish Messenger.
Observer (Presbyterian).
Tablet (Catholic).

Riding School—Fifth av. cor. 40th street.

Reading Rooms—Are in nearly all first-class hotels, with a large variety of newspapers.

Religion—Religion is fashionable in New York. The metropolis is filled with "popular preachers," who draw full houses, particularly on Sunday morning. The ministers have large salaries, and many of them are very wealthy.

Religious Statistics for the United States—The statistics of religion for the United States, just completed at the Census Office, show the total number of church organizations upon the 1st of June, 1870, to be 72,451; the total number of church edifices to be 63,074; the total church accommodation to be 21,659,562, and the aggregate value of the church property to be $354,429,581. The statistics of church accommodation for the principal denominations are as follows:—Baptist Regular, 3,997,116; Baptist, other, 363,019; Roman Catholic, 1,990,514;

Congregational, 1,117,212; Episcopal, 991,051; Lutheran, 997,332; Methodist, 6,528,209; Presbyterian, Regular, 2,198,900; Presbyterian, other, 499,344. The value of the Church property owned by these denominations is:—Baptist, regular, $39,229,221; Baptist, other, $2,378,977; Catholic, Roman, $60,985,566; Congregational, $25,069,698; Episcopal, $36,514,549; Lutheran, $14,917,747; Methodist, $69,854,121; Presbyterian, regular, $47,828,732; Presbyterian, other, $5,436,524.

[Bethel Church, or Seamen's Floating Chapel.]

STATISTICS—See Manual of the Corporation of New York.

It contains details of the institutions of the city; the State and Metropolitan Commissions, and the Government Departments of the city.

To be found in Corporation library, room **No. 12**, first floor, City Hall.

SATURDAY—Is a fashionable day for ladies to attend public entertainments—alone. These are advertised in the daily papers under the head of "Matinees." Handsome walking suits are worn. Gentlemen can of course attend these matinees either with or without ladies, but the number of ladies very far predominates.

SEAMEN'S CHAPELS—All along the North and East Rivers are chapels for seamen, of different denominations.

SILVER COMMUNION SERVICE, PRESENTED BY QUEEN ANNE—This is owned and used by Trinity Cathedral. The original church which stood on the site of the present edifice was the recipient of it.

SINGING IN CHURCHES—There is fine singing in most of the Protestant as well as the Catholic churches in the metropolis; solos by a lady *artiste* being considered a great addition to the service.

SHOOTING GALLERIES—The sign will attract the stranger as he goes along Broadway. He has only to enter, take his turn, and "pay the shot."

SHOPPING—Cheap goods are principally sought for in the Bowery, Third avenue, Grand street, Catharine street, and Division street, on the east side of town, and on the west side in Hudson, Carmine, and Bleecker streets; but those who live remote from these streets will generally find little advantage in going out of Broadway. Here, in the best known emporiums, goods can be found at fair prices, and but one price is asked. Very cheap goods are necessarily of inferior quality and fashion, and look so. These you do not find in Broadway.

SHOP BUTCHERS—These persons have a license to sell meats and vegetables, and have small markets wherever they choose to erect them in various parts of the city. These little markets are a great convenience.

STEAMBOAT TRAVEL—(See page 192.)

SHALL WE HAVE FLOWER SHOWS?—The suggestion is certainly a pleasing one, and all the necessary ingredients to its success are at hand. The flower shows of London are renowned for their popularity, and gain yearly in attractiveness and beauty. Why should not our own upper ten inaugurate the custom here? In the spring, just after the theatrical season is over, and before it is time to repair to the seaside and watering places, there comes a dull time here which the flower show just fits. Something light and graceful is needed, and an exhibition of spring flowers, aided by the attractions of music, sunshine, and soft air, is admirably the thing. In the fall another void in the social life appears. The first brisk winds of autumn depopulate the summer resorts, and yet the time for winter amusements is not quite come. Once more, a flower show meets the need. The spring has its odorous blossoms and the fall its gorgeous blooms.

SNOW BLOCKADE—Once in four or five years comes a snow blockade which impedes all kinds of locomotion, stops the trains about to leave the city, and fills to repletion every hotel, small and great, of every class. It furnishes great amusement to the young, and valuable occupation to the laborer.

STREET PROCESSIONS—These have always been a special feature in New York; all nationalities having been allowed free scope to display their banners and march through our streets, often to the great discomfort of business people or the interruption of travel. At last, owing especially to danger from the bitter feeling exhibited in the case of the Orange procession in 1871, the legislature interfered and regulated the affair of street processions, which are still free, but subject to proper restrictions. The bill provides for the freedom of the streets in which cars run, and the unobstructed passage of the cars, by declaring that "whenever any procession shall find it necessary to march across a railway track, the portion of said procession which in so marching is likely to stop the passage of any car or cars upon said track shall come to a halt in order to permit said car to proceed." The bill also forbids processions except of the National Guard, the Police, and the Fire Department, unless notice is given to the Police authorities, and the latter are empowered to designate to such procession or parade how much of the street in width it can occupy with special reference to crowded thoroughfares through which said procession may move. Sunday parades, excepting actual funeral processions, are forbidden.

SUBURBAN VILLAGES—Those within the city limits are Carmansville, Manhattanville, Yorkville, and Harlem. These are fast becoming continuous with the city.

Melrose, Morrisania, Tremont, Fordham, etc., are almost continuous in Westchester County—reached by Harlem Railroad Accommodation Train.

These are characteristic American villages of the more affluent type.

The suburban Long Island villages are Astoria, Flatbush, Flushing, Jamaica, Newtown, etc., etc. The Staten Island villages are seen to best advantage from the Bay. The residences from this point of view have a very picturesque effect. The neighboring villages in new Jersey are also fine places of resort in summer.

SHIPPING INTELLIGENCE—Is to be found minutely recorded in the daily papers.

TAKE THE RIGHT HAND side as you walk along the streets; also the right hand in riding or driving.

THOSE WHO WISH TO REMAIN for some time in the Metropolis and who desire to practise the strictest economy, had better apply at some of the first-class boarding-houses advertised in the daily papers. A small but comfortable bedroom can be had in one of these, with good meals, for ten or twelve dollars a week. Apply only where references are given and required.

TIME TABLES—At all the railroad depots in the city, and in the ferry-boats, and across the ferries at depots, are Time Tables nailed up on the walls of the waiting-rooms. As the hours of starting vary with the seasons, it is best to leave the travellers to consult these as to when, and at the same time how, to go to distant places.

The Time Tables contain a printed list of places near and distant on the railroad routes, marking the towns and villages at which each of the different trains stop, and at what hours; also the hours for starting from New York and the hours of leaving the aforesaid places, and of arrival from them in New York. These Time Tables will be found in all railway stations throughout the country, and are most explicit. One of them printed on paper can be had for the asking at the ticket office of the station in New York.

UNFURNISHED APARTMENTS—These are abundant for the lower and working classes in what are called "tenement houses." For the higher classes they are not so common, the latter finding their homes in hotels, boarding-houses, and in a whole private house. A new class of fashionable lodging-houses is, however, being introduced, but their success is still to be proved. The rates charged are exorbitant. The largest of the kind is the new Stevens Apartment Building.

UNDERGROUND RAILROAD.—This great work, which is to give rapid transit for the people of Westchester County to the lower part of the city, has been commenced and will be carried to a rapid completion. It is expected that the road will be finished before September 1, 1874. Commodore Vanderbilt is the leading spirit of the enterprise and altogether controls it.

TABLE OF DISTANCES.

FROM BATTERY.	FROM EXCHANGE.	FROM CITY HALL.	TO.
¼ mile.			Rector street.
½	¼ mile.		Fulton.
¾	½		City Hall.
1	¾	¼ mile.	Leonard.
1¼	1	½	Canal.
1½	1¼	¾	Spring.
1¾	1½	1	Houston.
2	1¾	1¼	Fourth.
2¼	2	1½	Ninth.
2½	2¼	1¾	Fourteenth.
2¾	2½	2	Nineteenth.
3	2¾	2¼	Twenty-fourth.
3¼	3	2½	Twenty-ninth.
3½	3¼	2¾	Thirty-fourth.
3¾	3½	3	Thirty-eighth.
4	3¾	3¼	Forty-fourth.
4¼	4	3½	Forty-ninth.
4½	4¼	3¾	Fifty-fourth.
4¾	4½	4	Fifty-eighth.
5	4¾	4¼	Sixty-third.
5¼	5	4½	Sixty-eighth.
5½	5¼	4¾	Seventy-third.
5¾	5½	5	Seventy-eighth.
6	5¾	5¼	Eighty-third.
6¼	6	5½	Eighty-eighth.
6½	6¼	5¾	Ninety-third.
6¾	6½	6	Ninety-seventh.
7	6¾	6¼	One Hundred and Second.
7¼	7	6½	One Hundred and Seventh.
7½	7¼	6¾	One Hundred and Twelfth.
7¾	7½	7	One Hundred and Seventeenth.
8	7¾	7¼	One Hundred and Twenty-first.
8¼	8	7½	One Hundred and Twenty-sixth.
8½	8¼	7¾	One Hundred and Thirty-first.
8¾	8½	8	One Hundred and Thirty-sixth.
9	8¾	8¼	One Hundred and Fortieth.
9¼	9	8½	One Hundred and Forty-fifth.
9½	9¼	8¾	One Hundred and Fiftieth.
9¾	9½	9	One Hundred and Fifty-fourth.

From Battery to King's Bridge (city limit), 15 miles.

WINES AND LIQUORS—These can be got of as good a quality as from the importers at a first-class retail grocery store. These stores are numerous in our principal thoroughfares, both up and down town. You can purchase these either by the box or single bottle.

WALL STREET SNEAK THIEVES have a new device by which to commit "sneak robberies." They lay some harmless explosive article on the floor, which when trodden on naturally attracts the attention of clerks and others. They take that opportunity to seize upon any valuables within reach.

WAITERS IN HOTELS—New York Hotel waiters are accustomed to being civilly spoken to, and are respectful accordingly. Here, as everywhere in the United States, only the under-bred and vulgar are arbitrary in manner towards servants.

[*Institution for the Blind—Ninth Avenue.*]

THE CENTRAL PARK.

[*Central Park—Summer House on the Lake.*]

CENTRAL PARK—Between Fifth avenue and Eighth avenue—East and West—and between 59th street and 110th street, North and South.

The Central Park was commenced in 1857.

At each gate of the Park is a gate-keeper. On the grounds are park-keepers. One of their duties is to give any necessary information to visitors. Lost articles are taken care of by a Property Clerk in the Old Arsenal.

See Index for "Cars," which go to the Park.

Gates open all day, at all seasons, and in summer from 5 a. m. to 11 p. m.

No fees permitted to any of the officials in the Park.

Central Park is one of the four largest parks in the world, and perhaps the most beautiful of all. It covers an area of about 850 acres, laid out in such varied beauty as to harmonize with the mood of the moment, and attract and satisfy all tastes. The stately drives, the rural walks, the commanding views, the

[*Central Park—The Upper Lake.*]

romantic dells—the bridges, the statues, the arches, the terrace, to attract the artistic eye—the pond, the dairy, the play-ground suggestive of juvenile sports and juvenile simplicity. The Mall, the Casino for the fashionable and the *bon vivant*—the lake with its boats, and the cave with its weird entrance for the sentimental dreamer.

The Maze, invented it would seem expressly for lovers, since its central point and egress are designedly left almost unattainable, of old fortifications, reminding one of sterner times, the streams, the cascades, suggestive of untrammelled nature.

[*Central Park—The Cave—Lower Lake.*]

The reservoir bringing the mind forcibly back to the practical fact of human progress, and the luxury of its perfected inventions. The Museum of Natural History, with all its wonders, and the Menagerie, and to render the combination complete, the perfect *abandon* which all—rich or poor—may enjoy in their rambles. It is a spot well worth coming a hundred miles to visit.

It would take up too much space to mention each object of attraction minutely, but the Park is open at all hours of the day, and to all.

On Saturday afternoons in summer, there is a fine band of music. The Music Pavilion is at the northern end of the Mall and not far from the Casino.

Carriages, provided by the Park Commissioners and accommo-

[*Central Park—Grotto leading to the Cave.*]

dating ten or a dozen persons, are to be found at the Fifth avenue and 59th street gate, and at the Eighth avenue and 59th street gate.

They leave at short intervals.—Fare 25 cents for each person.

New structures are constantly in progress of execution for ornamenting the Central Park and also for the convenience of visitors.

The Park, under the genial warmth of Spring and Summer suns fresh with green verdure, fostered with the moisture of gentle rains, makes a charming retreat for the residents of the city, tired and weary with their weekly labors in the densely populated business quarters. It is only on a fine Sunday that we can really appreciate the many charms of the Park, and understand the happiness and pleasure that its beautiful walks, picturesque *châlets* and refreshing limpid lakes afford to thousands of our fellow citizens. On week days the carriages of the rich roll along its level drives and children play about the smooth grass plats; but it is only on Sundays that Central Park becomes a really cosmopolitan resort. If the weather is fine all classes are there. The young aristocrat drives by in his showy dog-cart and tandem, and Hans, with his *frau*, six children, *frau's* mother and *frau's* brother, carrying an ample basket containing the lunch, come in a party to breath the fresh air and enjoy the afternoon.

There are Cottages for ladies placed in different parts of the grounds, in charge of a female attendant.

Entrances to the Central Park.

The Scholars' Gate, Fifth avenue and 59th street.
The Artists' Gate, Sixth avenue and 59th street.
The Artisans' Gate, Seventh avenue and 59th street.
The Merchants' Gate, Eighth avenue and 59th street.
The Women's Gate, Eighth avenue and 72d street.
The Hunters' Gate, Eighth avenue and 79th street.
The Mariners' Gate, Eighth avenue and 85th street.
The Gate of All Saints, Eighth avenue and 96th street.

The Boys' Gate, Eighth avenue and 100th street.
The Children's Gate, Fifth avenue and 72d street.
The Miners' Gate, Fifth avenue and 79th street.
The Engineers' Gate, Fifth avenue and 90th street.
The Woodman's Gate, Fifth avenue and 96th street.
The Girls' Gate, Fifth avenue and 102d street.
The Pioneers' Gate, Fifth avenue and 110th street.
The Farmers' Gate, Sixth avenue and 110th street.
The Warriors' Gate, Seventh avenue and 110th street.
The Strangers' Gate, Eighth avenue and 110th street.

BRIEF HISTORY OF OLD NEW YORK.

PASSING over Scandinavian traditions, which contain accounts of the landing of the Norsemen on our continent some time before the expedition of Christopher Columbus, we give but slight credit to the statement of some, that the site of the present city of New York was actually visited by an early navigator named Verazzano, in the year 1524.

The earliest authentic account is that of the voyage of Henry Hudson (frequently written Hendrick Hudson), an Englishman in the service of the Dutch East India Company. The European world was still intent on a North-East passage to India. Hudson, who was not only an intelligent, but a bold and fearless navigator, had induced English enterprise to test his theory for two successive years. His friends then became discouraged and Hudson abandoned England for Holland, which country at that period enjoyed a commercial supremacy.

It is well settled that Hudson, in the "Half Moon," dropped anchor in the Bay of New York on the 3d of September, 1609. Pushing up the noble river which now bears his name, he came to the "Tappan See," where the river widens into a bay, and had his faith confirmed that he was on the right course for China. This confidence was soon weakened as he entered the Highlands, but he persevered till he reached Albany, when he abandoned all idea of the feasibility of his project and returned down the river and back to Amsterdam.

We reject the story (with many others) of the purchase of as much land by the whites of the Indians as the hide of a bullock could encompass, and of the cutting it into slender thongs so that it reached over a goodly portion of the island. The tale is taken almost literally from Virgil, and refers to the purchase of Carthage :—

> "The wandering exiles bought a space of ground
> Which one bullhide enclosed and compassed round."
> *Æneid*, Book 1, 490-1.

That Hudson inspired the natives with a friendly feeling is indicated by the name given to the spot—Manahachtanienks—said to mean "place where all got drunk;" from this comes "Manhattan," by which the island is even now designated. A still better evidence is in the fact that the Dutch in the following year, 1610, sent vessels to open a trade with the natives and a settlement was almost immediately commenced.

So admirable a site for a town was not destined to remain in the peaceful possession of the first discoverers. The English, inheriting the old Saxon love of right by the strong arm, soon pounced on the enviable locality. Argal, Governor of Virginia, returning from a raid on the French settlements in Acadia, put into New Amsterdam, surprised the honest Dutch governor, Christiaensen, and compelled a surrender of the place to the King of England. But the Dutch rallied in force the following year, retook the place and fortified it, and the same year, 1614, Holland made a "grant" of the whole country under the title of New Netherland. Under this possession it was long held and known. No important event took place till the reign of Charles II. king of England. In 1664 that monarch, disregarding the rights, claims, and settlements of the Dutch, granted all New Netherland to his brother James, then Duke of *York* and *Albany*, afterwards the noted James II. of England, who was virtually expelled from the English throne and was succeeded by "William and Mary."

An expedition was fitted, consisting of four frigates and 300 soldiers, to take possession under the grant of Charles; and on the 27th August, 1664, the city of New Amsterdam capitulated to the English, and on the 24th of September Fort Orange made a similar submission. *In commemoration of the titles of the Duke, who was the grantee of the patent, New Amsterdam was named New York, and Fort Orange, Albany.* In 1667, by the treaty of Breda, New Netherland was confirmed to the English, and as a compensation Surinam was ceded to the Dutch.

But the English occupation was not to exist without its reverses. In 1673 a Dutch war broke out, and a small squadron sent by them, after committing ravages in Virginia, came to New York and demanded surrender not only of the town but of all the country. This was assented to without a shot being fired on either side, and the Dutch once more took possession. The very next year, peace was made between England and Holland. New Netherland was restored to the English, and the English territories in Guiana to the Dutch. The Duke of York confirmed his title by a new patent, and Andreas was made governor. The first legislative assembly was held under governor Dougan, in 1683. New York suffered greatly from the arbitrary rule of James, but in 1689 William and Mary came to the English throne and restored New York to its lawful privileges. In 1692 special attention began to be turned towards the fortifications.

In 1698 the Earl of Bellomont was made governor. From his speech to the Legislature it would seem that New York rulers have inherited the practice of plundering the city. The Earl says: "I cannot but observe to you what a legacy my predecessor has left me and what difficulties to struggle with; a few miserable, naked, half-starved soldiers, *not half the number the king allowed pay for.*" Much more follows in the same vein, from which we conclude that human nature was pretty much the same then as in the days of our " Ring."

The English now felt secure of their rich possessions.

A free grammar-school was started in 1702, which seems for

years to have sufficed, so far as free schools were concerned. In 1725 the first newspaper was issued, and in 1732 a free Classical Academy was founded. New York now began to rapidly improve and increase. Business of every kind flourished, and the city assumed a more vigorous aspect.

In the troubles with the mother country which some years after succeeded, and which culminated in the war of the Revolution, New York took a firm and undaunted stand. But the city was too great a prize for the English not to lay out all their forces to possess. The unfortunate issue of the battle of Long Island made it impossible for General Washington to hold New York. The result was, that the city with all its fortifications and appurtenances fell into the hands of the British fleet and army under Admiral and General Howe, September, 1776. For a little more than seven years—in fact till the end of the war—the English held possession of the town. On the 25th of November, 1783, they evacuated it, and Washington and the Governor of the State made their triumphal entry. Ten years later New York had doubled its population.

From the completion of the Erie Canal, in 1825, may be dated the new era of commercial prosperity and grandeur for this metropolis. She now soon outstripped her rival in population—Philadelphia—and has continued to increase in almost fabulous proportions. In October, 1842, the Croton Aqueduct was completed, supplying the only serious need of the city.

New York, though a very healthy place, has been thrice visited by a very severe pestilence. In 1795 by yellow fever, and in 1832 and again in 1849 by Asiatic cholera. The city has suffered from two fires of almost unexampled extent—one in 1835, and the other in 1845. Nothing, however, has served apparently even to check the growth of this metropolis.

Sites of Remarkable Events.

The brilliant assemblies of the "Court of Washington" were held in the old City Hotel between Pine and Cedar streets.

"The Old Sugar House," converted into a prison for American soldiers, by the British, stood in Liberty street, near the old post-office.

Washington's residence stood at the North angle of Franklin square. Here he held his State receptions.

Washington Irving was born in one of a row of houses, and at about the centre of the block, in William street, between John and Fulton.

At the corner of Charlton and Varick streets, once lived successively, Washington, John Adams, and Aaron Burr.

At the Bowling-green stood once a Dutch and English Fort.

On the site of the United States Treasury was once a pillory and whipping-post.

On the same site, in the Hall of Legislature, George Washington was elected the first President of the United States.

Col. Alexander Hamilton lived in a neighboring house.

The stamps were burned in 1776, where Catharine street now stands.

Talleyrand, when ambassador to the United States, lived on the site of the Metropolitan, the large building between Prince and Houston streets, east side Broadway.

Washington's farewell interview with his officers took place at a tavern corner Pearl and Broad streets.

At No. 1 Broadway, lived successively during the Revolution, Lord Cornwallis, Gen. Clinton, Lord Howe, and Gen. Washington.

Fulton died in a house on this site. The traitor Arnold here concocted his nefarious projects.

OLD NEW YORK ADVERTISEMENTS.

To be Sold, a good, likely Negroe Man, about 22 years of Age, is an extraordinary cook, and understands all Manner of House work. Enquire of the Printers here of.—*The New York Gazette: or the Weekly Post-Boy*, July 9, 1753.

To be Let. Bedloe's Island, alias Love Island, together with the Dwelling House and Light House, being finely situated for a tavern, where all kind of Garden Stuff, Poultry, &c., may be easily raised for the Shipping outward bound, and from where any Quantity of pickled Oysters may be obtained; it abounds with English Rabbits.—*Ibid.*

Travelers are desired to observe, in going from Flat-Bush to said Ferry (Yellow Hook ferry), to keep the mark'd trees on the right hand.—*New York Mercury*, June 18, 1753.

Just imported in the Ship Fame, Capt. Seymour, from Hamburgh, and to be Sold on board the said Vessel, by JOSEPH HAYNES or said Master; A parcel of very likely, healthy PALATINES, of all Trades. As also Women and Children, &c.—*Ibid.*

To-Morrow will be Published (Price 1s.), And sold by the Printer hereof; The Tragedy of CATO, by Mr. Addison.—*Ibid.*

Notice is hereby given that Abraham Webb, being provided with a Boat exceeding well fitted, with a very handsome Cabbin, and all necessary accomodations; proposes to give his attendance, at the White Hall Slip, every Monday and Thursday; and the same Day, Wind and Weather permitting, to proceed for Amboy Ferry to John Cluck's, where a Waggon,

Kept by John Richards, will be ready to receive either Goods or Passengers, and to proceed with them to Borden's Town, where a Stage Boat will be ready to carry them to Philadelphia; and the same method will be followed from the Crooket Billet Wharf at Philadelphia, up to Borden's Town, and shall proceed Load or no Load, twice a Week, by which Means, Passengers or Goods may never be detained on the Road. As they purpose to endeavour to use People in the best Manner they are capable of, they hope all good Persons will give it the encouragement it deserves. So with Respect they remain Friends to the Publick.—*The New York Gazette: or the Weekly Post-Boy,* June 4, 1753.

[*Bloomingdale Lunatic Asylum—117th street.*]

BROOKLYN.

BROOKLYN, which has a population of nearly half a million, is the third city in size in the United States, ranking next to Philadelphia. It is separated from New York only by the East river, and is as much a part of the metropolis, as the "Surrey Side" is of London. The Brooklynites have steadily resisted being incorporated with their larger neighbor, though they have themselves swallowed Williamsburgh—now called "Brooklyn E. D."—East District. Brooklyn has been termed the "lodging-house of New York," because probably nine-tenths of the wealthy residents do business in the city. Nevertheless, the inhabitants feel very independent of the metropolis, and are ambitious of rivalling it. The numerous ferries which cross every two or three minutes make access between the two places very easy, and the great bridge soon to be completed will add to the facility of intercommunication.

PUBLIC BUILDINGS.

CITY HALL—One mile from Fulton Ferry, and is opposite the junction of Fulton and Court streets.

POST OFFICE—Washington street, near the junction of Myrtle avenue and Fulton street.

CITY ARMORY—Corner Henry and Cranberry streets.

LONG ISLAND COLLEGE HOSPITAL—Henry st., near Pacific.

CITY HOSPITAL—Raymond st., near Dekalb av.

There are in Brooklyn Asylums, various Institutes, and Dispensaries, Banks, Lyceums, and all other accessories of a large city. The Mercantile Library numbers forty-one thousand volumes.

MARINE HOSPITAL—Wallabout Bay

STATE ARSENAL—Corner Portland avenue and Auburn Place.

ACADEMY OF MUSIC—Montague street, between Court and Clinton streets.

KINGS COUNTY JAIL—Raymond street, Fort Green.

ACADEMY OF DESIGN—The increasing popularity and success of the semi-annual exhibitions of the Brooklyn Art Association demanded a larger and more suitable room than the Assembly Room of the Academy of Music. The Association therefore have erected a building that contains ample accommodation for the exhibitions and the School of Design. It is next to the Academy of Music.

The exterior, which is ornate, is of tinted stone, the buff stone from Scotland, and the red freestone from Ohio. The arches over the entrance and windows are delicately sculptured in the forms of birds, reptiles, ferns, etc. From the main entrance a tower rises into a picturesque gable to the height of one hundred and ten feet from the sidewalk. This tower contains the vestibule and main stairway. The interior walls are finished in buff pressed brick relieved by bands of Philadelphia brick and Ohio sandstone. The stairway is built of oak with mahogany trimmings. No soft wood is used in the building. The basement is devoted to the use of the schools of the Academy of Design. The grand gallery on the second floor is very fine. Opening out of this hall is a water-color gallery and a sculpture-room. An arched doorway opens from the main gallery into the assembly-room of the Academy, thus giving abundance of wall space for the pictures and of floor for the guests on reception nights. Studios are above.

The chronological collection embraces works representative of American art, as far as it was possible to obtain them, from 1715 to the present time.

Charles Wilson Peale, one of our earliest American artists, is represented by two portraits, one of Washington and one of

Franklin. The last sitting for this portrait was but eight days before the death of Franklin, and it is unfinished.

At one end of the gallery is Gilbert Stuart's full-length portrait of Washington, painted in 1794.

Opposite the Stuart portrait hangs Trumbull's portrait of Washington, considered the finest one in existence.

PUBLIC WORKS.

UNITED STATES NAVY YARD, situated on Wallabout Bay. See Index for "Ferries."

ATLANTIC DOCK, South Ferry. Take Hamilton Ferry, foot White Hall street, N. Y.

PROSPECT PARK—A new park of immense size, which promises to rival even Central Park in extent and artificial adornments. It commands beautiful views. It is well wooded. It can be reached by horse-cars starting from the ferries.

GREENWOOD CEMETERY—A couple of miles from South Ferry. Omnibuses carry you there from the ferry. It is at the present time one of the largest and perhaps the most beautiful cemetery in the world; it commands, also, splendid views of city and harbor. Free admission on week-days, etc. Permits obtainable at any undertaker's.

WATER WORKS—The resources of the Brooklyn Water Works are said to be six times as great as those of New York. The water is supplied from Rockville Lake, Hempstead, L. I., and also from Ridgewood.

CARS—There are cars starting from all the ferries for all parts of Brooklyn.

CHURCHES OF BROOKLYN AND PROMINENT PREACHERS.

PLYMOUTH CHURCH, CONGREGATIONALIST—Orange street, between Henry and Hicks streets. Rev. Henry Ward Beecher

CHURCH OF THE PILGRIMS, PRESBYTERIAN—Corner Remsen and Henry streets. Rev. Dr. Storrs.

BROOKLYN.

The DUTCH REFORMED CHURCH, in Pierrepont street, is a particularly beautiful church.

Church named CHURCH OF THE HOLY TRINITY, Episcopal—Corner Clinton and Montague streets.

GRACE CHURCH, Episcopal—Hicks street, near Remsen.

Church named CHURCH OF THE SAVIOUR, Unitarian—Corner Pierrepont street and Munroe place.

DUTCH REFORMED CHURCH—Rear of the City Hall. Rev. Dr. Dwight.

METHODIST CHURCH—Clinton street near Atlantic street. Rev. Dr. Cuyler.

From the numerous religious edifices in Brooklyn, that city has acquired the name of "The City of Churches."

HOTELS OF BROOKLYN.

The best hotel is the PIERREPONT HOUSE, Montague place, opposite Wall street Ferry.

The MANSION HOUSE, Henry street, near Pierrepont street, and the GLOBE HOTEL, 242 Fulton street, are also first-class hotels.

STEAMBOAT TRAVEL.

THE following is a complete list, alphabetically arranged, of the steamboats which ply between this city and points on the Hudson River, East River, Long Island Sound, New York Bay and New Jersey. None of these boats make a Sunday trip unless specially mentioned.

ALBANY—New Jersey Steamboat Company, "People's Line." One of the fine steamboats of the line—Drew or Dean Richmond—will leave Pier 41 North River, foot of Canal street, at 6 P. M. daily, connecting at Albany with railroads, North, East and West; returning from Albany at 7 P. M. daily, or on the arrival of connecting trains.

ALBANY AND TROY DAY-BOATS—Landing at Catskill, Cornwall, Cozzens', Hudson, Tivoli, Newburgh, Nyack, Poughkeepsie, Rhinebeck, Tarrytown, West Point and Yonkers. Steamboats D. Drew and C. Vibbard leave Pier 39 North River at 8:30 A. M., landing at 34th street.

ALBANY, TROY AND CATSKILL—New York and Troy Steamboat Company's steamboats Connecticut and Vanderbilt, leave Pier 44 North River at 6 P. M. daily, Saturdays excepted, connecting at Albany with railroads, North, East and West. Returning, leave Troy at 6 P. M., and Albany at 7 P. M., Saturdays excepted.

ALBANY, TROY, AND CATSKILL—Steamboats Sunnyside and Thomas Powell, leave Pier 43 North River daily, Saturdays excepted, at 6 P. M., connecting at Albany with railroads North. Returning, leave Troy daily, Saturdays excepted, at 6 P. M.

Athens, Tarrytown, Catskill, Tivoli, Hyde Park, Staatsburg, Smith's Dock, Rhinebeck, Germantown, Malden and Stuyvesant—Propeller Andrew Harder leaves Pier 35 North River, Tuesdays, Thursdays and Saturdays, at 5 p. m. Returning, leaves Athens, Mondays, Wednesdays and Fridays, at 5 p. m.

Astoria, L. I.—Steamboats Sylvan Glen and Sylvan Stream, Sylvan Dell and Sylvan Grove, daily, from Pier 24 East River, at 6:30, 8, 9 and 10 a. m.; 12 m.; 1, 3, 4, 5, 6:15, 7 p. m. Returning, leave Astoria at 6:15, 7:15, 8:15, 9:15, 10:15, 11:15 a. m.; 2:15, 3:15, 4:15, 5:15, 6:15 p. m. *Sunday Arrangement.*—Boats leave Harlem at 8:30 a. m. and hourly and half-hourly thereafter during the day, landing at Astoria and Eleventh street, each trip. Last boat leaves Harlem at 7:30 p. m. and Peck slip at 8:15 p. m. This is the only line connecting with the regular line of boats for High Bridge. Passengers by this line of boats can visit the Government Works at Hell Gate, Schneider's and Schutzer's Parks at Astoria, Christ Park and Karl's Park at North New York, and High Bridge.

Baylis's Dock, L. I. (Fort Schuyler)—Steamboat Seawanhaka daily, from Pier 24 East River, at 4 p. m., calling at Thirty-third street each way. Returning, leaves Baylis's Dock at 8:20 a. m.

Bay Ridge, L. I.—Steamer Bay Ridge, from Wall street ferry at 8.30 and 11 a. m.; 2, 4, 5:15 and 6:30 p. m. Returning, leaves Bay Ridge at 8, 9:10 a. m., and 12:45, 2:35 and 4:35 p. m.

Bergen Point, N. J.—Steamboat Chancellor at 11 a. m. and 4:30 p. m. daily, from Pier 14 North River. Returning, leaves Bergen Point at 8:25 a. m. and 2:25 p. m.

BOSTON—Steamboats Bristol and Providence, daily, from Pier 28 North River at 5 P.M. Returning trains leave Old Colony and Newport Railway Depot, Boston, at 5:30 P.M., connecting at Fall River.

BOSTON—Steamboats Electra and Metis, daily, from Pier 27 North River at 5 P.M. Returning train leaves Boston at 2 P.M.

BOSTON—Steamboats Stonington and Narragansett daily, from Pier 33 North River at 5 P.M. Returning trains leave Boston from Boston and Providence Railroad Depot, at 5:30 P.M.

BOSTON—Steamboats City of Boston and City of New York, daily, from Pier 40 North River at 5 P.M. Returning train leaves from Boston, Hartford and Erie Railroad Depot, foot of Summer street, at 6:15 P.M.

BRIDGEPORT, CONN.—Steamboats Bridgeport and J. B. Schuyler, daily, at 12 M. and at 12 midnight, from Pier 35 East River. Returning, leave Bridgeport daily, except Saturdays, at 9 A.M. and 11 P.M.

BRIDGEPORT, Conn.—Steamboats Artisan at 11:30 A.M., and Wyoming at 4 P.M. Returning, leave Bridgeport at 7:25 A.M. and 11:30 P.M.

COLD SPRING, CORNWALL, FISHKILL, HAVERSTRAW, NEWBURGH, LOW POINT, MARLBOROUGH, AND NEW HAMBURG—Steamers Walter Brett and River Queen leave Pier 43 North River at 4:30 P.M. Returning, leave New Hamburg daily, except Saturdays, at 7 P.M.

CATSKILL, SMITH'S DOCK, HYDE PARK, STAATSBURG, COLD SPRING, RHINEBECK, TIVOLI, MALDEN, WEST CAMP, GERMANTOWN, &c.—Steamboat Neversink, from Pier 35 North River at

6 P.M. Tuesdays, Thursdays and Saturdays. Returning, leaves Catskill at 6 P.M. Mondays, Wednesdays and Fridays.

COLLEGE POINT—Steamboat Osseo, daily, except Sunday, from Pier No. 22 East River at 10 A.M. and 4 P.M. Returning, leaves College Point at 8 A.M. and 1:15 P.M.

COXSACKIE, ATHENS, GERMANTOWN AND MALDEN.—Steamer Monitor leaves Pier 49 North River on Monday, Wednesday and Friday at 5 P.M. Returning, leaves Coxsackie on Tuesday, Thursday and Sunday at 4 P.M.

COXSACKIE.—Steamer Redfield leaves Pier 51 North River on Tuesday, Thursday and Saturday at 5 P.M. Returning, leaves Coxsackie on Monday, Wednesday and Friday at 4:30 P.M.

ELIZABETHPORT, N. J.—Steamboats Chancellor and Kill Von Kull, at 11 A.M., 4:30 P.M. and 5 P.M. daily, from Pier No. 14 North River Returning, leave Elizabethport at 6:45 and 8 A.M. and 2 P.M.

FALL RIVER, MASS.—Steamboats Bristol and Providence from Pier No. 28 North River at 5 P.M. daily. Returning, leave Fall River at 7 P.M.

FORT LEE AND PLEASANT VALLEY—Pleasant Valley, from Pier No. 43 North River at 10 A M., 2 and 5:15 P.M., calling at Thirty-fourth street each way.

FLUSHING. L. I.—Steamboat Osseo, daily from Pier 22 East River at 10:50 A.M. Returning, leaves Flushing at 12:40 P.M.

GLEN COVE, GLENWOOD, MOTT'S DOCK, GREAT NECK, SEA CLIFF GROVE, WHITESTONE, SANDS' POINT, AND ROSLYN, L. I.— Steamboat Seawanhaka, at 4 P.M., from Pier 24 East River, calling at 33d street each way. Returning, leaves Glen Cove at 7:40 A.M.

GLEN COVE, SEA-CLIFF GROVE, SANDS' POINT AND WHITESTONE, L. I.—Steamboat Arrowsmith, from Pier 24 East River at 9:15 A.M. Returning, leaves Glen Cove at 1:45 P.M., calling at 33d street each way.

GREENPORT, NEW SUFFOLK, SAG HARBOR AND ORIENT, L. I.— Steamboat Escort. Tuesday, Thursday, and Saturday, from Pier 4 North River, at 5 P.M. Returning, leaves Greenport Monday, Wednesday, and Friday at 5:30 P.M.

HARLEM AND YORKVILLE, N. Y. (landing at 11th and 120th street.)—Steamboats Sylvan Stream, Sylvan Dell, and Sylvan Grove daily, from Pier 24 East River (Peck Slip) at 7, 7:30, 8, 9, 9:30, 10, 11:30 A.M., 12 M., 1, 1:30, 3, 3:30, 4, 5, 5:30, 6:15, 7 P.M. Returning, leave Harlem at 6, 6:30, 7, 8, 8:30, 9, 10, 10:30, 11 A.M., 12:30, 2, 2:30, 3, 4, 4:30, 5, 6 P.M.

HARTFORD, MIDDLETOWN, AND CONNECTICUT RIVER LANDINGS— Steamer State of New York or Granite State, from Pier 24 East River (Peck Slip) daily at 4 P.M. Returning, leave Hartford daily, at 4 P.M., Sundays excepted.

HAVERSTRAW—Landing at Yonkers, Englewood, Nyack, Tarrytown, Hastings, Dobb's Ferry, and Sing Sing. Steamer Adelphi, from Pier 34 North River at 4 P.M. daily. Returning, leaves Haverstraw at 6:20 A.M.

HIGH BRIDGE AND KINGSBRIDGE—Connect at Harlem with boats from Pier 24 East River.

HUDSON—Nupha and Redfield, from Pier 51 North River, at 6 P.M. Returning, leave Hudson daily, except Saturday, 7 P.M.

KEYPORT, N. J.—Steamboat Matteawan, daily, from Pier 26 North River at 4 P.M. Returning, leaves Keyport at 7 A.M.

LONG BRANCH, N. J.—Steamboats Magenta or Gen. Sedgwick, daily, from Pier 28 North River at 6:40 and 9:40 A.M. 4 and 5 P.M. Returning, leave Long Branch at 7:40 and 10:33 A.M. and 6:05 P.M.

MARINERS' HARBOR—Steamer Chancellor at 11 A.M. and 4:30 P.M., from Pier 14 North River. Returning, leaves Mariners' Harbor at 7, 8, 10 A.M., and 2:10 P.M.

MORRISANIA, ASTORIA AND HARLEM (landing at 8th and 119th streets each way)—Steamboats Morrisania and Harlem, daily, from Pier 22 East River, at 7:15, 8:15, 9:15, 10:15, A.M.; 1:15, 3:15, 4:15, 5:15, 6:20 P.M. Returning, leave Morrisania 6:5, 7:15, 8:15, 9:20, 10:15 A.M., 1:30, 2:45, 4:15, 5:15 P.M.

NEWARK—Thomas P. Way, from Pier 26 North River at 10:30 A.M. and 4:30 P.M. daily. Returning, leaves Newark at 7:15 A.M. and 1 P.M.

NEW BEDFORD, MASS.—Steamers Acushnet and Wamsutta, Wednesday and Saturday, from Pier 13 East River at 3 P.M. Returning, leave New Bedford Wednesday and Saturday at 2 P.M.

NEW HAVEN, CONN.—Steamboats Elm City, daily at 3:15 P.M.; City of Hartford, at 11 P.M., Saturday night at 12, from Pier 25 East River. Returning, leave New Haven at 10:15 A.M. and 11 P.M. Steamer New Haven leaves New Haven for New York Sunday nights only, at 11 o'clock.

NEW LONDON, CONN.—Steamboats City of Boston and City of

New York, daily, from Pier 40 North River at 5 P.M. Returning, leave New London at 10:30 P.M.

NEW LONDON, CONN.—Steamboats City of Lawrence and City of Norwich, daily, from Pier 40 North River at 5 P.M. Returning, leave New London at 9:30 P.M.

NEWPORT, R. I.—Steamboats Providence and Bristol, daily, at 5 P.M. from Pier 28 North River. Returning, leave Newport at 8 P.M.

NORWALK, CONN.—Nelly White, from Pier 37 East River, daily, at 2:45 P.M., and Thirty-third street at 3 P.M. Returning, leaves Norwalk at 7:45 A.M.

NORWICH, CONN.—Steamboats City of Lawrence and City of Norwich, daily, from Pier 40 North River at 5 P.M.

NYACK.—Landing at Yonkers, Hastings, Irvington, Dobbs' Ferry, Carmansville, Englewood, and Tarrytown—Alexis, from Pier 34 North River at 5 P.M. Returning, leaves Nyack at 6:15 A.M.

OYSTER BAY.—Calling at Bayville, Huntington, Jones' Dock, Laurelton, City Island, and Cold Spring—D. R. Martin, from Pier 37 East River, daily, at 4 P.M. Returning, leaves Oyster Bay at 6:30 A.M., calling at Thirty-third street both ways.

PEEKSKILL.—Calling at Yonkers, Dobbs' Ferry, Tarrytown, Nyack, Sing Sing, Haverstraw, Verplanck's and Grassy Point—Steamer Antelope, from Pier 34 North River, daily, Sundays included, at 8 A.M., and Thirty-fourth street at 8:15 A.M. Returning, leaves Peekskill at 1:30 P.M., arriving in New York at 5.30 P.M.

PEEKSKILL.—Landing at Yonkers, Irvington, Tarrytown, Nyack, Rockland Lake, Haverstraw, Grassy Point and Verplanck's

—The Chrystenah, from Pier No. 34 North River at 3:45 P.M. Returning, leaves Peekskill at 6:30 A.M.

PERTH AMBOY, ROSSVILLE AND STATEN ISLAND SOUND LANDINGS.—Steamboat Matano, daily, from Pier No. 13 North River at 3 P.M. Returning, leaves Perth Amboy at 7:05 A.M.

PORT WASHINGTON, WHITESTONE AND GREAT NECK, L. I.—Steamboat Arrowsmith, from Pier 24 East River at 5 P.M. Returning, leaves Port Washington at 6:45 A.M.

POUGHKEEPSIE, NEWBURGH, CORNWALL COZZENS', NEW HAMBURG, MILTON, RONDOUT AND WESTPOINT.—Steamer Mary Powell leaves Pier 39 North River at 3:30 P.M. Returning, leaves Rondout at 5:30 A.M.

POUGHKEEPSIE.—Landing at Marlboro', Highland, and New Hamburg—J. L. Hasbrouck and D. S. Miller, from Pier No. 35 North River at 5 P.M. Returning, leave Poughkeepsie at 7 P.M.

PROVIDENCE, R. I.—Electra and Meta, daily, from Pier 27 North River, at 5 P.M. Returning, leave Providence at 5:30 P.M.

RED BANK AND NEW JERSEY HIGHLANDS.—Steamboat Helen leaves Pier 35 North River daily, according to tide.

RONDOUT—Landing at Cozzens', Cornwall, Newburgh, Milton, Poughkeepsie and Esopus—James W. Baldwin or Thomas Cornell, daily, from Pier No. 34 North River at 4 P.M. Returning, leave Rondout daily, except Saturdays, at 6 P.M.

SAG HARBOR, L. I.—Steamer Escort, Tuesday, Thursday and Saturday, from Pier 26 East River at 5 P.M. Returning, leaves Sag Harbor Monday, Wednesday and Friday at 4 P.M.

SAUGERTIES AND TIVOLI—Steamboat Ausonia, Pier 49 North River, Tuesdays, Thursdays and Saturdays, at 5 P.M. Returning, leaves Saugerties Mondays, Wednesdays and Fridays, at 6 P.M.

SOUTH AMBOY, N. J.—Steamboat William Cook, daily, from Pier 1 North River at 4 P.M. (See Camden and Amboy Railroad.) Returning, leaves South Amboy at 10 A.M.

STATEN ISLAND FERRY—(North Shore)—Steamboats Pomona and Thomas Hunt, and Castleton, from Pier 19 North River for New Brighton, Port Richmond and Elm Park, every hour from 7 A.M. to 12 M., and from 2 P.M. to 7 P.M.

STATEN ISLAND RAILROAD FERRY—(South Shore)—Boats leave foot of Whitehall street for Vanderbilt Landing hourly, from 6 A.M. until 7 P.M. Returning from Vanderbilt Landing from 6 A.M. to 7 P.M., and at 10 P.M.

STAMFORD AND GREENWICH—Steamer Nelly White, from Pier 37 East River, daily, at 3:30 P.M., calling at 33d street. Returning, leaves Stamford at 7 A.M.

STONINGTON, CONN.—Steamboats Stonington and Old Colony, daily, from Pier 33 North River, at 5 P.M. Returning, leave Stonington at 9 P.M.

WESTCHESTER—UNIONPORT—Steamboat Osseo, daily, from Pier 22 East River, at 4:15 P.M. Returning, leaves Westchester at 7:15 A.M.

SUBURBAN RESORTS.

Valuable Facts as to the Places Neighboring New York.

WE present below a carefully compiled exhibit of the railroad stations within a radius of fifty miles around this city, together with other collateral figures of general interest. The rates of commutation on the Hudson and Harlem roads are given approximately; those of the New Haven road are in accordance with the schedule of reductions recently made—on one or two other roads there are no rates obtainable. For all practical purposes, however, the list will be found complete enough.

PLACES.	Distance.	Time.	Yearly Commutation.	Railroads.	Trains daily.
Allendale	26	1.45	$76 00	Erie	11
Avenel	23	1.00	77 50	New Jersey	6
Amityville	29	1.53	85 00	South Side	7
Brick Church	13	.53	69 00	Mor. & Essex.	16
Bloomfield	11	.59	69 50	Mor. & Essex.	13
Bayonne	5	.28	50 00	N. J. Central.	26
Bergen Point	7	.30	50 00	N. J. Central.	32
Bound Brook	27	1.35	95 00	N. J. Central.	14
Belleville	11	.41	62 50	Erie	7

SUBURBAN RESORTS.

PLACES.	Distance.	Time.	Yearly Commutation.	Railroads.	Trains daily.
Bogota.............	13	.43	.....	Midland.......	4
Bronxville...........	15	1.00	64 00	Harlem	6
Bedford	39	1.47	105 00	Harlem	4
Brookdale...........	19	.40	104 00	Flushing......	4
Bay Side............	16	.31	94 00	Flushing......	6
Broadway...........	14	.29	80 00	Flushing......	6
Baldwinsville........	19	1.20	75 00	South Side...	8
Belmore............	23	1.38	75 00	"	6
Breslau.............	32	2.00	85 00	"	6
Babylon............	35	2.06	90 00	"	7
Bay Shore..........	40	2.12	46 00	"	4
Chatham...........	25	1.35	82 00	Mor. & Essex.	9
Convent............	29	1.43	90 00	"	4
Clifton	13	.58	63 00	"	4
Communipaw.......	2	.15	45 00	N. J. Central..	26
Claremont..........	2½	.17	45 00	"	19
Centreville..........	6	.27	50 00	"	26
Crawford...........	15	.59	70 00	"	16
Clifton	14	.48	63 00	Erie	12
Carlstadt	9	.42	60 00	"	8
Cherry Hill.........	15	1.03	75 00	"	9
Cresskill...........	17	1.09	.....	North N. J...	7
Closter.............	19	1.17	.....	"	9
Corrieville	22	1.23	.....	"	4
Campgaw...........	29	1.29	.....	Midland......	5
Crystal Lake........	30	1.32	.....	"	5
Charlotteburg.......	43	1.54	.....	"	4
Central Morrisania...	7	0.27	44 00	Harlem.......	12
Chappaqua..........	32	1.30	90 00	"	3
Croton Falls........	48	2.10	250 00	"	4
Croton	34	1.26	111 00	Hudson	6
Cruger's............	37	1.33	114 00	"	6
Cos Cob............	29	1.23	95 00	New Haven...	10
College Point........	13	0.23	72 00	Flushing......	21
Creedmore Range...	17	0.36	90 00	Flushing.,....	4
Centerport..........	38	1.50	98 00	Long Island...	3
Denville	38	1.50	98 00	M. & E.......	5

PLACES.	Distance.	Time.	Yearly Commutation.	Railroads.	Trains daily.
Dunellen	24	1.25	90 00	N. J. Central..	10
Demarest	18	1.13	.....	North N. J...	8
Dundee Lake	18	0.57	.....	Midland	6
Dobb's Ferry	20	0.52	100 00	Hudson	9
Darien	38	1.40	105 00	New Haven...	7
Douglaston	16	0.36	98 00	Flushing	5
Deer Park	36	1.54	.....	Long Island..	2
East Orange	11	0.48	68 00	M. & E.	16
Elizabethport	8	0.39	60 00	N. J. Central.	30
Elizabeth	12	0.47	65 00	" & N. J.	70
Englewood	14	1.00	.....	North. N. J...	9
East Newark	8	0.28	65 60	New Jersey...	10
Evona	23	1.21	87 50	N. J. Central.	5
Fanwood	20	1.10	80 60	"	14
Finderne	31	1.40	100 00	"	9
Franklin	13	0.47	63 00	Erie	7
Fairview	8	0.43	25 00	North N. J...	7
Fordham	9	0.38	60 00	Harlem	14
Fort Washington	5	0.24	52 00	Hudson	13
Five Mile River	39	1.43	110 00	New Haven...	4
Fort Montgomery	45	1.59	100 00	Hudson	2
Flushing	12	0.25	68 00	Flushing	20
Far Rockaway	20	1.03	75 00	Long Island..	4
"	20	1.30	80 00	South Side....	4
Farmingdale	30	1.26	85 00	Long Island...	2
Freeport	21	1.25	75 00	South Side...	7
Greenville	3	0.20	45 00	N. J. Central.	26
Granton	7	0.37	.....	North. N. J...	6
Greenwood	44	2.38	109 25	Erie	1
Golden Bridge	44	1.57	111 00	Harlem	4
Glenwood	15	0.41	76 00	Hudson	5
Garrisons	49	2.03	112 00	"	7
Greenwich	29	1.18	90 00	New Haven...	10
Green's Farms	49	2.02	125 00	"	5
Garden City	22	0.42	100 00	Flushing	5
Glen Cove	28	1.28	100 00	Long Island..	4
Glen Head	26	1.20	95 00	"	4

SUBURBAN RESORTS.

PLACES.	Distance.	Time.	Yearly Commutation.	Railroads.	Trains daily.
Glendale............	5	0.30	50 00	South Side...	6
Huntley............	21	1.21	78 00	M. & E......	4
Hawthorne.........	19	1.22	67 50	Erie........	6
Hoboken...........	24	1.39	72 25	"	11
Highland...........	15	0.53	63 50	"	7
Highland Mills......	49	2.03	118 75	"	4
Hillsdale...........	21	1.27	108 00	"	9
Homestead.........	5	0.32	.....	North. N. J...	7
Houtenville........	22	1.00	75 00	New Jersey...	5
Hackensack........	13	0.45	.....	Midland......	8
Harlem............	4	0.15	28 00	Harlem.....	15
Hart's Corners......	20	1.15	88 00	"	6
Hastings...........	19	0.44	96 00	Hudson......	8
Harrison...........	22	0.58	80 00	New Haven...	8
Hempstead.........	24	0.50	100 00	Flushing......	8
Hempstead.........	22	1.09	75 00	Long Island..	6
Hinsdale...........	18	0.38	90 00	Flushing......	8
Hyde Park.........	20	0.43	95 00	"	6
Hyde Park.........	17	0.59	75 00	Long Island..	5
Hicksville..........	25	1.12	80 00	" ..	5
Huntington........	35	1.45	96 00	" ..	3
Inwood............	5	0.28	60 00	Hudson......	13
Irvington..........	22	0.57	108 00	"	8
Islip...............	43	2.17	47 00	South Side...	4
Jamaica...........	10	0.30	60 00	Long Island..	7
Jamaica...........	8½	0.45	60 00	South Side...	8
Jerusalem.........	28	1.18	85 00	Long Island..	2
Kingsland.........	8	0.41	60 00	Morris & E...	4
Kinder Kamock.....	19	1.18	96 00	Erie.........	8
Katonah...........	42	1.49	108 00	Harlem......	4
Lafayette..........	..	0.15	45 00	New'k & N. Y.	10
Lake View.........	16	0.56	64 25	Erie.........	12
Lodi...............	12	0.50	63 50	"	9
Leonia.............	11	0.53	.....	North. N. J...	8
Linden.............	18	1.00	65 60	New Jersey...	13
Larchmont.........	18	0.50	75 00	New Haven...	3
Little Neck........	17	0.40	98 00	Flushing......	6

PLACES.	Distance.	Time.	Yearly Commutation.	Railroads.	Trains daily.
Lawrence............	18	0.58	75 00	Long Island..	4
Locust Valley.......	30	1.30	100 00	" ...	2
Lakeland............	48	2.27	.....	" ...	2
Locust Avenue......	10½	0.50	60 00	South Side...	5
Lawrence............	19	1.25	80 00	South Side...	4
Montrose............	15	1.02	71 00	M. & E......	16
Maplewood..........	17	1.09	73 00	"	7
Milburn.............	19	1.15	75 00	"	12
Madison.............	17	1.38	85 00	"	8
Morristown..........	31	1.45	90 00	"	9
Morris Plains........	34	1.50	93 00	"	5
Montclair............	11	1.05	71 00	"	15
Mountain View......	21	1.25	80 00	"	2
Mawah..............	30	1.56	81 50	Erie.........	7
Monroe..............	50	2.58	123 75	"	8
Marion	3	0.20	45 00	N. J.........	16
Meulo Park..........	24	1.05	75 00	"	5
Metuchen............	26	1.12	75 00	"	3
Middlebush..........	37	1.51	85 00	"	4
Maywood............	15	0.47	...	Midland......	6
Midland Park.......	25	1.16	....	"	7
Mott Haven.........	5	0.19	32 00	Harlem......	14
Melrose.............	6	0.24	36 40	"	14
Morrisania..........	7	0.27	40 00	"	14
Mount Kisco........	37	1.41	96 00	"	4
Mount St. Vincent...	13	0.37	76 00	Hudson......	13
Montrose............	38	1.37	120 00	"	6
Mount Vernon.......	14	0.37	70 00	New Haven..	10
Mamaroneck........	20	0.54	80 00	" ..	10
Mineola.............	20	1.00	75 00	Long Island..	6
Merrick	23	1.30	75 00	South Side...	8
Newark	9	0.40	65 60	M. & E......	30
"	9	0.36	60 00	Erie.........	8
"	9½	0.35	65 60	New Jersey...	43
New Milford........	17	1.11	87 00	Erie.........	8
New Durham.......	6	0.35	....	Nor. N. J....	6
Norwood............	21	1.21	....	"	7

SUBURBAN RESORTS.

PLACES.	Distance.	Time.	Yearly Commutation.	Railroads.	Trains daily.
Nanuet............	31	1.30	....	Nor. N. J....	3
New Brunswick.....	32	1.29	85 00	New Jersey..	21
Newfoundland......	44½	2.00	....	Midland.....	4
New Rochelle.......	17	0.47	105 00	New Haven..	11
Norston...........	37	1.37	105 00	"	6
Norwalk (So.)......	2	1.48	115 00	"	13
Newton............	9	0.17	64 00	Flushing.....	11
Northport.........	40	2.00	100 00	Long Island..	3
North Islip	43	2.12	....	"	2
N. Belleville........	12	0.44	26 50	Erie.........	7
Orange Junction.....	12	0.50	68 50	Morris & E...	16
Orange	14	0.56	69 50	"	17
Orange Valley.......	14½	0.59	70 00	"	16
Oradell............	18	1.14	89 00	"	8
Orangeburg.........	25	1.15	....	Nor. N. J....	3
Oakland...........	31½	1.35	....	Midland......	5
Oak Ridge.........	45¼	2.05	....	"	2
Ocean Pond........	17	0.56	75 00	Long Island..	4
Ocean Point........	18	1.22	80 00	South Side...	4
Oakdale...........	47½	2.22	....	"	4
Passaic............	11	0.53	62 25	Morris & E...	4
"	12	0.44	62 25	Erie.........	17
Paterson...........	15	1.00	65 00	Morris & E...	6
"	17	1.00	65 00	Erie.........	22
"	20	1.00	....	Midland......	8
Pamrapo...........	4	0.23	45 00	N. J. Central.	26
Plainfield..........	22	1.05	85 00	"	18
Piermont...........	27	1.35	....	North. N. J..	7
Perth Amboy........	27	1.24	75 50	New Jersey..	6
Pompton	34½	1.43	....	Midland......	6
Purdy's............	45¾	2.06	120 00	Harlem.......	3
Peekskill..........	45	1.46	120 00	Hudson......	11
Pelhamville.........	16	0.41	70 00	N. Haven....	6
Port Chester........	26	1.11	85 00	"	11
Queens............	13	0.38	65 00	Long Island..	6
Roseville	11	0.45	66 00	Morris & E...	22
"	11	0.50	66 00	"	11

PLACES.	Distance.	Time.	Yearly Commutation.	Railroads.	Trains daily.
Rockaway, N. J.....	40	2.08	100 00	Morris & E...	5
Ridgewood..........	11	1.02	70 00	"	14
"	22	1.32	71 00	Erie.........	11
Rutherford Park....	9	0.45	60 00	Morris & E...	4
" "	10	0 37	60 00	Erie.........	17
Roselle.............	14	0.54	65 00	N. J. Central.	16
Ramsey's.........	28	1.51	71 50	Erie.........	10
Ramapo............	34	2.08	87 00	Erie.........	6
River Edge........	16	1.08	82 75	Erie.........	8
Rahway............	20	1.04	75 00	New Jersey..	17
Ridgefield Park.....	11	0.33	....	Midland.....	6
Rochelle............	16	0.50	....	"	7
Riverside...........	21	1.04	....	"	5
"	30	1.24	95 00	New Haven..	10
Riverdale...........	12	0.36	72 00	Hudson......	16
Rye...............	24	1.05	85 00	New Haven...	10
Rowayton..........	39	1.43	110 00	"	4
Roslyn.............	24	1.14	95 00	Long Island..	4
Richmond Hill......	7	0.37	50 00	South Side...	7
Rockville Centre....	17½	1.15	75 00	"	7
L..dgewood, L. I.....	25	1.40	75 00	"	6
South Orange.......	16	1.04	72 00	Morris & E...	17
Summit............	22	1.25	78 00	"	12
Somerville..........	33	1.45	100 00	N. J. Central.	12
Suffern.............	32	2.02	83 25	Erie.........	10
Sloatsburg..........	36	2.15	90 75	Erie.........	5
Southfields.........	42	2.30	104 50	Erie.........	6
Sparkill............	24	1.31	....	Nor. N. J....	9
Spring Valley.......	33	1.37	....	"	3
South Elizabeth.....	15¼	0.55	65 60	New Jersey..	15
Spa Springs........	25	1.19	77 50	"	6
Stelton............	29	1.19	75 00	"	3
Smith's Mills........	39	1 58	....	Midland......	3
Snufftown..........	49¾	2.10	....	"	4
Scarsdale...........	19	1.11	80 00	Harlem......	6
Spuyten Duyvil.....	11	0.31	68 00	Hudson......	15
Scarborough........	29	1.14	99 00	"	8

SUBURBAN RESORTS.

PLACES.	Distance.	Time.	Yearly Commutation.	Railroads.	Trains daily.
Sing Sing............	30	1.20	99 00	Hudson......	10
Stamford............	34	1.29	100 00	N. Haven....	17
So. Norwalk........	42	1.48	115 00	"	13
Southport..........	50	2.07	125 00	"	6
Syosset.............	29	1.26	95 00	Long Island..	3
St. Johnsland.......	45	2.18	103 00	" ..	3
Smithtown...:......	49	2.26	105 00	" ..	3
Springfield..........	11¾	0.54	60 00	South Side...	7
So. Oyster Bay......	27	1.45	80 00	" ...	7
Sayville	50	2.25	52 00	" ...	4
Turner's............	48	2.50	117 75	Erie	12
Tenafly,............	16	1.05	....	Nor. N. J....	9
Tappan.............	23	1.26	....	"	8
Tallman's...........	37	1.45	....	"	3
Tremont............	7¾	0.33	48 00	Harlem.....	14
Tuckahoe...........	16	1.03	64 00	"	6
Tarrytown..........	25	1.06	112 00	Hudson......	10
Uniontown..........	23	1.03	75 00	New Jersey..	4
Unionville..........	28¼	1.17	90 00	Harlem......	3
Van Winkle's........	23½	1.12	...	Midland.....	5
Voorhees...........	35	1.44	85 00	New Jersey..	4
Valley Stream.......	14¾	1.05	75 00	South Side...	8
Watsessing..........	11	0.56	69 50	M. & E......	12
Whitehall.	25	1.38	90 00	"	2
Westfeld............	17	1.05	75 00	N. J. Central.	18
Woodside...........	10	0.39	62 00	Erie	7
Woodbridge.........	10	0.46	60 75	Erie	8
"	23	1.13	77 50	New Jersey..	6
Westwood	20	1.23	102 00	Erie	9
Waverley...........	12	0.45	65 60	New Jersey.	13
Wortendyke.........	26	1.20	....	Midland......	8
Wyckoff............	27¼	1 23	....	"	5
Williamsbridge......	10½	0.44	64 00	Harlem......	14
Woodlawn..........	12	0.48	64 00	"	5
West Mt. Vernon....	13¼	0.45	64 00	"	9
White Plains........	22½	1.13	100 00	"	9
Westport	45	1.57	120 00	N. Haven.....	6

PLACES.	Distance.	Time.	Yearly Commutation.	Railroads.	Trans daily.
Whitestone..........	15	0.34	78 00	Flushing......	21
Winfield............	8½	0.15	60 00	"	12
West Flushing......	10	0.19	64 00	"	11
Woodside...........	8	0.12	56 00	"	12
Westbury...	22	1.05	80 00	Long Island..	5
Woodsburg..........	17¼	1.18	80 00	South Side...	4
Yonkers............	15	0.45	66 00	Hudson......	14

GILSEY HOUSE,

Corner Broadway and 29th Street,

[NEW YORK.]

EUROPEAN PLAN.

BRESLIN, GARDNER & CO.

METROPOLITAN HOTEL,

BROADWAY,

BETWEEN HOUSTON AND PRINCE STREETS,

[NEW YORK.]

BRESLIN, PURCELL & CO.

GRAND UNION HOTEL,

[Saratoga Springs,]

OPEN JUNE 1st, 1873,

FOR RECEPTION OF GUESTS.

Application for Rooms can be made to either of the above Hotels.

Knickerbocker

LIFE INSURANCE COMPANY.

239 BROADWAY,

Cor. Park Place.   NEW YORK.

CHARLES STANTON, Pres.   GEORGE F. SNIFFEN, Sec.
JOHN A. NICHOLS, 2d Vice-Pres. CHARLES M. HIBBARD, Actuary.

ASSETS, OVER $8,000,000.

This Company now issues policies on its new Savings Bank Plan—the best, safest, and most satisfactory system in use.

These Policies Guarantee a Surrender Value,

cannot be misunderstood, and are commended by the leading actuaries of the country.

SEWING MACHINES.

The sales of Sewing Machines in 1872, as reported under oath, in 1873, to the owners of the Sewing Machine Patents, show that the

SINGER MANUFACTURING CO.

LAST YEAR SOLD

219,758 Machines,

OR, 38,948 MORE THAN IN 1871,

90 Per Cent. of them being for Family Use.

THIS IS OVER

45,000

More Sewing Machines than were sold by any other company during the same period, and over ONE QUARTER of all the Machines sold in 1872.

PRINCIPAL OFFICE OF

THE SINGER MANUFACTURING CO.,

34 UNION SQUARE, NEW YORK.

www.ingramcontent.com/pod-product-compliance
Lightning Source LLC
Chambersburg PA
CBHW031832230426
43669CB00009B/1319